PRAISE FOR GUN VIOLENCE 101

"Illustrator Violet Lemay and criminologist Tom Gabor are the dream team we've been waiting for. Their collaboration of bold illustration alongside straightforward truth-telling provides a vital resource for gun violence resistance. This book will save lives."

—Caroline Light, director of Program in Women, Gender, and Sexuality Studies at Harvard University and author of *Stand Your Ground: A History of America's Love Affair with Lethal Self-Defense*

"This is the book that every American should read to understand why we have gun violence and what we must do to move forward and solve it."

—uttenberg, Parkland dad and National Spirit Award winner

"Creative, informative, and powerful… *Gun Violence 101* literally illustrates the magnitude of the problem in a manner that is both unique and accessible."

—Louis Klarevas, research professor at Columbia University Teachers College and author of *Rampage Nation: Securing America from Mass Shootings*

"*Gun Violence 101* is visually appealing and incredibly easy to read and understand. It should be required reading for all members of Congress, state legislators, and other lawmakers."

—Po Murray, founder of Newtown Action Alliance

"*Wow*! I absolutely *love it*! It is appealing to the eye, very easy to read, and has very interesting facts with cool pictures… I know this will appeal to upper elementary and middle school students."

—Ron Hobert, president of the American Federation of Teachers Kansas

"Gun violence is everywhere, and Gabor explains why in as clear-headed a fashion as can be imagined. This thoughtfully illustrated book is sensible, helpful, and above all, sane."

—Robert J. Spitzer, Distinguished Service Professor at SUNY Cortland and author of *The Politics of Gun Control* (9th ed.), *The Gun Dilemma*, and *Guns Across America*

"What a wonderful resource for educators and the general public. Just so easy to read and comprehend via visuals. There are specifically so many members of gun violence prevention organizations that would benefit from reading this book… You truly only need this book to read and understand the complexities in an easy format… Thank you, Tom and Violet. Outstanding work."

—Patricia Hatch, founding member and former president of Cape Cod Grandmothers Against Gun Violence

GUN VIOLENCE 101

GUN VIOLENCE 101

A Graphic Guide to How Gun Safety Policies Save Lives

Thomas
Gabor, PhD

Violet
Lemay

MIAMI

Copyright © 2025 by Thomas Gabor, PhD and Violet Lemay.
Published by Mango Publishing, a division of Mango Publishing Group, Inc.

Cover, Layout & Design: Fred Fruisen & Violet Lemay
Cover Illustration: Violet Lemay

Mango is an active supporter of authors' rights to free speech and artistic expression in their books. The purpose of copyright is to encourage authors to produce exceptional works that enrich our culture and our open society.

Uploading or distributing photos, scans or any content from this book without prior permission is theft of the author's intellectual property. Please honor the author's work as you would your own. Thank you in advance for respecting our author's rights.

For permission requests, please contact the publisher at:
Mango Publishing Group
5966 South Dixie Highway, Suite 300
Miami, FL 33143
info@mango.bz

For special orders, quantity sales, course adoptions and corporate sales, please email the publisher at sales@mango.bz. For trade and wholesale sales, please contact Ingram Publisher Services at customer.service@ingramcontent.com or +1.800.509.4887.

Gun Violence 101: A Graphic Guide to How Gun Safety Policies Save Lives

Library of Congress Cataloging-in-Publication Number: 2024949721
ISBN: (print) 978-1-68481-746-7, (ebook) 978-1-68481-747-4
BISAC: POL077000 POLITICAL SCIENCE / Public Policy / Gun & Firearm Policy

Printed in the United States of America

"FIREARM VIOLENCE IS AN URGENT PUBLIC HEALTH CRISIS THAT HAS LED TO LOSS OF LIFE, UNIMAGINABLE PAIN, AND PROFOUND GRIEF FOR TOO MANY AMERICANS."

—Dr. Vivek Murthy
US Surgeon General under
President Joseph R. Biden

CONTENTS

FOREWORD by Fred Guttenberg, National Spirit Award Winner......................................x

PREFACE..xiv

1 **AMERICA'S PRIVATE ARSENAL**....................1

2 **GUN DEATHS AND TRAUMA:**
The US vs. the World................................13

3 **GUN LAWS IN AMERICA:** A Brief History.....25

4 **GUN CULTURE IN AMERICA**..........................33

5 **GUNS DO KILL:** The Weapon Matters...............47

6 **LETHALITY OF TODAY'S WEAPONS**...........55

7 **SELF-DEFENSE:** Reality or Illusion?.....................65

8 **MASS SHOOTINGS:** Random, Targeted,
or Reckless?..79

9 **DO GUNS MAKE WOMEN SAFER?**................87

10 **ROOTS OF GUN VIOLENCE**: How Important Is Mental Illness?..93

11 **THE CONSTITUTION**: Are Gun Rights Unlimited?..105

12 **THE GUN INDUSTRY**..................................115

13 **PUBLIC OPINION ON GUNS AND VIOLENCE**..129

14 **SUICIDE**: Do Methods Matter?...................135

15 **DO GUN LAWS WORK?**............................143

16 **A DECLARATION OF THE RIGHT OF AMERICANS TO LIVE FREE FROM GUN VIOLENCE** Drafted by Thomas Gabor...............155

ACKNOWLEDGMENTS..............................160

NOTES...162

ABOUT THE AUTHOR & ILLUSTRATOR.......174

FOREWORD
by Fred Guttenberg, National Spirit Award Winner

I woke up the morning of February 14th, 2018, ready for a new beginning. Four months prior, on October 17th, 2017, my brother Michael had died of cancer related to his service in 9/11 where he ran the triage for the WTC bombing site. My family had never experienced loss like this before. As part of the process of moving my family forward from grief, I had a plan to make a big deal out of this Valentine's Day. As holidays go, Valentine's Day was always my wife's favorite holiday and my daughter Jaime was also becoming a fan, even though she was only 14. On this Valentine's Day, I had a plan to introduce my kids to the romance of the day by taking my old VHS wedding video and digitizing it so that we could watch it as a family after school. I will never forget that morning as I could not wait for my kids to leave for school so that I could get to work on our special Valentine's Day. I was busy rushing my kids out the door. You have to go; you're going to be late, I told them. I was so busy telling them to go, I never actually told them how much I loved them that morning. Of course, I assumed I would get that chance many times during that day. I was only sending them to school, a place to safely learn. Later that day, my son Jesse called to say, "Hey dad, there is a shooter at my school." This day changed my life and my family forever. My children were in the Parkland school shooting. My son Jesse came home that day. My daughter Jaime did not.

One year prior to this shooting, I had sold my business. At the time of the shooting, I was looking for something new to do. For me, it was not about just income. For the first time in my adult life, I did not have a purpose, and I needed one. This shooting that resulted in the murder of my daughter and 16 others gave me a purpose and a mission that has guided me ever since. Following 9/11, which was very personal to me, I watched as America came together to protect all of us from foreign terrorism. Following my daughter's murder and all other instances of gun violence, I watched as America broke into sides. There were those affected by gun violence and amazing activists and organizations who wanted to do anything possible to stop future acts of gun violence. However, it was clear that the gun lobby had a way of discussing gun violence and dominating the conversation. It became clear to me that the gun lobby had perfected the ability to turn every act of gun violence into an opportunity to sell more weapons. It was also clear that facts and data were not a part of the discussion for them. They used fear, intimidation, and marketing slogans designed to sell more guns as a response to gun violence. Something needed to change.

Following my daughter's murder, I got to know many amazing people working hard to reduce gun violence. One of those people is Tom Gabor. As many may know, in 2023, Tom and I published our book *American Carnage*. We researched and addressed all of the myths around gun violence with facts and data. We provided readers an easy and understandable way to talk about gun violence and to understand why we are seeing increasing levels of gun violence. It was time to reclaim this conversation from the gun lobby. Following our very first interview of the media tour for our book on *Deadline: White House* with Nicolle Wallace, Tom and I became acquainted with Violet Lemay, who posted illustrations of Tom and me from our interview online. The result of that introduction resulted in conversation and ultimately this incredible collaboration between Tom and Violet.

Anyone who knows me has heard me say, "Understanding and solving gun violence is not rocket science." In fact, I believe that understanding its causes and what to do next is easy. However, it requires facts and data and the ability to distinguish between facts and lies. The lies and myths are what had always made this such a complicated problem to solve. This new book from Tom and Violet takes the work of *American Carnage* and brings it to a new level of understanding as it combines facts and data with incredible illustrations. This is the book that every American should read to understand why we have gun violence and what we must do to move forward and solve it.

For me, I wish this book had existed before my family became a family affected by gun violence. Perhaps if it had, I would have become better informed then and worked harder to stop gun violence before it affected my family. For those of you already affected, this is your textbook for understanding and activism. For those of you not yet affected by gun violence, this is the book that you must read to better understand the issue and to understand why it matters to you. Thank you, Tom and Violet, for writing this truly incredible and important book.

PREFACE

This illustrated book is unique in presenting core facts about gun violence through an equal reliance on text and visuals, such as original artwork and graphics. It is the product of a special collaboration between Thomas (Tom) Gabor and Violet Lemay, two individuals with very different backgrounds and skill sets. Tom, lead author of the 2023 bestseller *American Carnage: Shattering the Myths That Fuel Gun Violence*, has worked as a criminology professor, researcher, expert witness, and international gun violence consultant for 40 years. Violet has illustrated over 40 books and written seven, including *Alithia Ramirez Was an Artist*, an award-winning picture book biography of an Uvalde, Texas gun violence child victim who was an aspiring artist.

America is beset with unprecedented levels of gun violence. Gunfire now accounts for nearly 50,000 fatalities a year and the number of mass shootings has doubled over what they were in the 2010s, with an average of nearly two per day. Over half of all Americans have been personally touched by gun violence and close to a third avoid certain public settings due to the fear of getting shot.

Misinformation on gun violence, much of it promoted by the gun lobby and its allies, poses a major challenge to gun law reform as some Americans have been influenced by their campaign to convince the public that guns in the home, gun carrying, and permissive laws, such as those allowing gun carrying without a permit, will make the country safer. There are real-world consequences to this campaign as more Americans are carrying guns on a daily basis, many more are purchasing assault weapons today, and more gun owners are keeping their firearms loaded and accessible in the home. These trends have had a catastrophic effect on American society. The misinformation spread by those who stand to profit from the chaos must be challenged with facts based on the most recent, credible research.

Through non-technical language and illustrations, this book is intended for students, activists, and the general public who need to become better acquainted with all the myths surrounding gun violence and exposed to the promising strategies available to combat the scourge. It is an easy read compared with a heavy, text-laden volume. For many people, visuals can be easier to call to mind than verbal arguments. A key aim of this book is to provide memorable visuals that will promote debate and discussion out in the world.

Surveys of youth and the growth of groups like Students Demand Action show how widespread the concern is about gun violence. There are literally hundreds of thousands of gun violence activists in the US. Activists are very passionate about this issue, as many have lost family members and/or friends to gun violence. We are in awe of their passion, but they must also be well informed.

As seen in these photos from a Midwestern truck stop, there is no shortage of visually engaging pro-gun messages. Regardless of their merit, these bumper sticker slogans display the potential influence and reach of illustrations in spreading a message. An easy-to-read, illustrated book may be what is needed to "arm" activists with the knowledge they need in the struggle for gun law reform. Informing activists is critical in enhancing the credibility of the gun violence prevention movement, countering arguments of the gun lobby, helping activists deal with the press, and in effectively lobbying legislators.

The combination of text, graphics, and original artwork will help readers digest the contents of this book while being exposed to important issues such as: gun ownership levels in the US, the history of gun regulation, the importance of lethal weapons in violence, prevalence of assault weapons, the frequency with which guns are used for self-defense, the meaning of the Constitution's Second Amendment, public opinion on gun violence, and effective solutions to the problem.

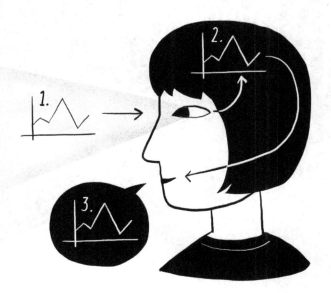

Visuals can be easier to recall.

This book will build on *American Carnage* and other books that counter the National Rifle Association's 40-year campaign to promote an armed citizenry and a "guns everywhere" agenda. This book continues the work of laying out a factual foundation that takes on the sea of misinformation on gun violence. Policy reform will then follow. The ultimate aim is to achieve what most of us seek—a society in which kids can attend school safely and people can work and enjoy leisure activities in their communities without the fear of getting shot or losing loved ones.

"FEW AUSTRALIANS WOULD DENY THAT THEIR COUNTRY IS **SAFER** TODAY AS A A CONSEQUENCE OF GUN CONTROL."

—*John Howard*
former Prime Minister of Australia who led national reforms

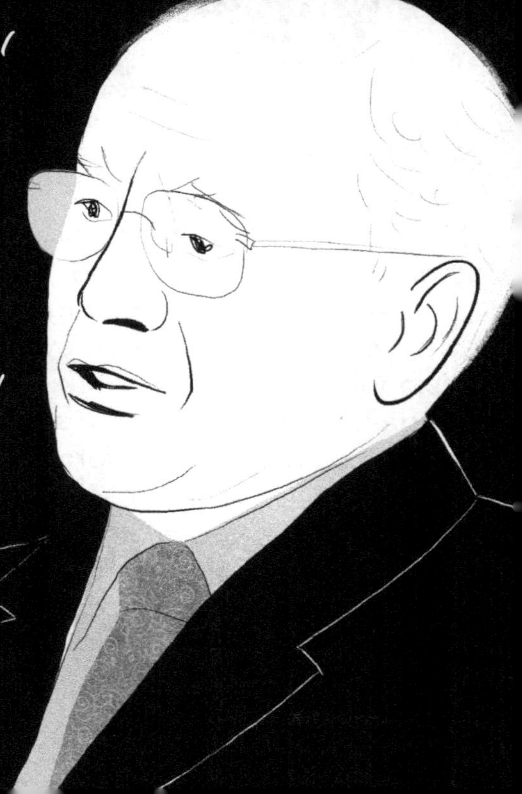

1

AMERICA'S PRIVATE ARSENAL

Americans own approximately 400 million firearms—close to half of the world's privately-held firearms—despite accounting for just 4 percent of the planet's eight billion people. America's private arsenal is startling as the US has more guns than people, with many owning numerous guns.

A GLOBAL OUTLIER

The US has the most armed civilian population in the world, with 120 guns for every 100 people. By contrast, Indonesia and Japan have fewer than one privately-held firearm for every 100 people.

TOP 10 COUNTRIES FOR CIVILIAN FIREARM HOLDINGS

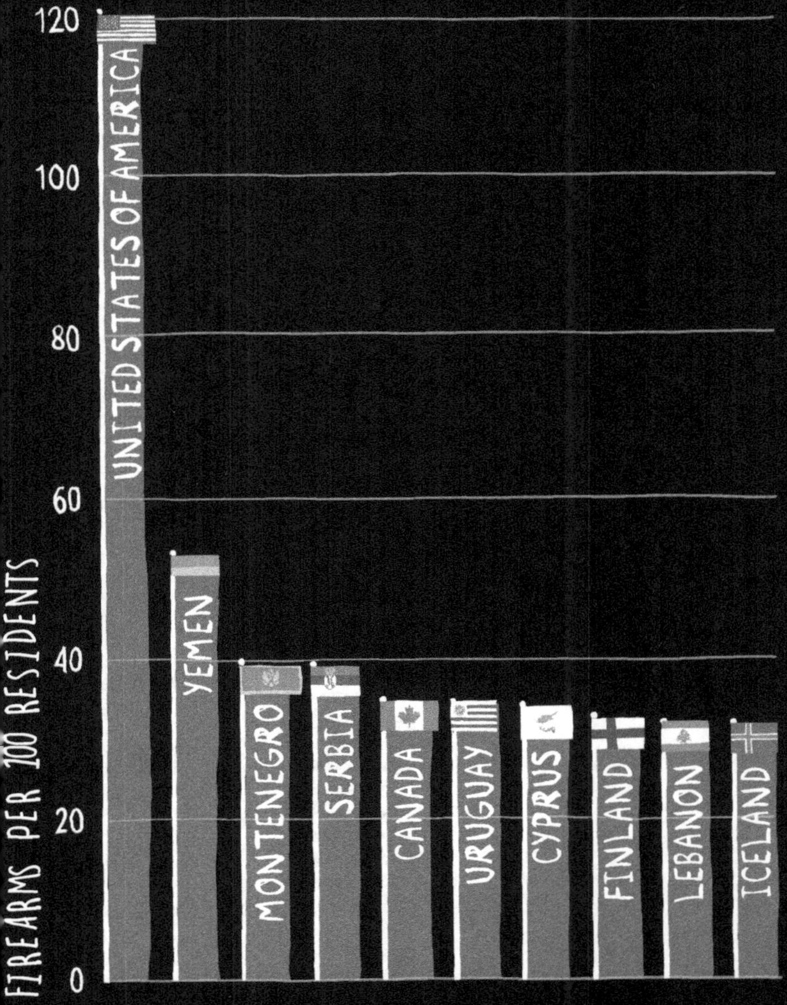

FIREARMS PER 100 RESIDENTS
0
20
40
60
80
100
120
UNITED STATES OF AMERICA
YEMEN
MONTENEGRO
SERBIA
CANADA
URUGUAY
CYPRUS
FINLAND
LEBANON
ICELAND

WEAPONS OF WAR

The US stands alone in failing to impose a national ban on or restrict weapons, like the AR-15, that were designed for war. The number of assault rifles in civilian hands has increased from 400,000 in the mid-1990s to about 20 million today.

Mid 1990s   2023

20,000,000

15,000,000

10,000,000

5,000,000

KEY — 400,000 Assault Rifles

0

BACKGROUND CHECK SYSTEM

The National Instant Criminal Background Check System (NICS) is just that; typically a two-minute check of three FBI databases to see whether a person buying a gun from a licensed dealer has a criminal conviction, mental illness, or other status disqualifying him from purchasing a firearm. Those buying guns privately through the internet or gun shows need not undergo a background check—the so-called

PRIVATE-SALE LOOPHOLE.

Also concerning is that if no disqualifying condition is found within three business days, the sale proceeds by default. In some cases, a gun is sold before law enforcement can make a final determination regarding the eligibility of a buyer to acquire a firearm. This is known as the Charleston Loophole, following a case in which the system wasn't able to verify the criminal record of an individual who subsequently committed a mass shooting at a Charleston (South Carolina) church.

As no checks are conducted beyond the FBI databases, disturbing behavior that does not result in a criminal conviction usually will not be entered in these databases and individuals such as the 2018 Parkland, Florida school shooter, who issued threats and displayed numerous disturbing behaviors, can purchase their weapon legally. In addition, many states fail to send complete information to the FBI regarding a resident's juvenile record, drug offenses, and mental health issues. Several states require a permit to purchase a firearm or increase the time law enforcement has to conduct a background check.

Most advanced countries require a license before an individual can purchase or possess a firearm. Consider federal law in Australia, a country that revamped its gun laws significantly following a major mass shooting in 1996.

BUYING GUNS IN AUSTRALIA

Australia has a history of gun ownership and a powerful gun lobby. Still, gun laws are far stricter than in the US.

- Unlike the US, there is no legal right to a gun
- Most automatic and semiautomatic firearms have been banned
- Firearms like the AR-15 are restricted to military, police, and certain pest controllers
- Owners must first obtain a license and establish a "genuine need" for a firearm
- Self-protection is not considered a genuine reason to possess or own a firearm
- Licensing procedures include gun safety training, proof of safe storage compliance, criminal & mental health checks
- A minimum 28-day waiting period for firearm purchases, allowing authorities to complete appropriate background checks
- Sales must go through licensed dealers
- Firearms are registered with police
- High caliber & easily concealable handguns are prohibited

CARRYING GUNS IN THE US

Aside from the number of guns and assault-style weapons in civilian hands, the US is also an outlier with regard to its highly permissive laws relating to the carrying of guns. All states now allow the carrying of concealed firearms and all but a few allow open carry in some form. Over half the states and counting now allow people to carry guns without a permit, meaning there is no requirement of a criminal background check, training in marksmanship and the safe handling of a gun, or education on when it is legally permissible to use lethal force.

Contrast this situation with Canada, a country that is far from having the strictest gun laws among advanced countries.

CARRYING GUNS IN CANADA

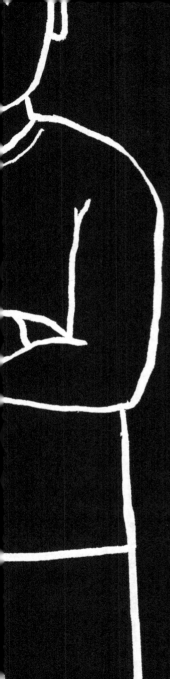

- Handguns are classified as restricted weapons & are registered with the national police agency
- Owners need a firearms license & must pass a test in gun safety & the law
- Safe storage requirements apply to all firearms
- Guns cannot be carried without a special license due to an occupational need (e.g., security work) or for self-protection where there is a verifiable threat to a person's life

FIREARM STORAGE IN THE US

Unlike most advanced countries, the US has no national laws requiring gun owners to store their guns in a specific manner to avoid their misuse. About five million American children live in homes in which firearms are loaded and unlocked. As Americans today are more likely to acquire guns for self-protection than for hunting or sport shooting, many keep guns loaded and in an accessible place. Unsecured firearms are a major source of weapons used in school shootings, youth suicides, and unintentional shooting deaths involving children.

Contrast the situation in the US with Germany, which tightened its gun laws following three major school shootings in the early 2000s.

FIREARM STORAGE IN GERMANY

- Guns must be stored separately from ammunition, unless they are stored in a secure container
- Persons possessing firearms must provide authorities with proof of measures taken for their secure storage
- Owners must grant authorities access to places where weapons are stored to ensure compliance with storage requirements
- Where there is an urgent threat to public safety, the authorities may enter living areas against the owner's will
- Individuals violating safe storage requirements may incur fines of up to 10,000 Euros

"IF IT'S NOT A HEALTH PROBLEM, THEN WHY ARE ALL THOSE PEOPLE **DYING** FROM IT?"

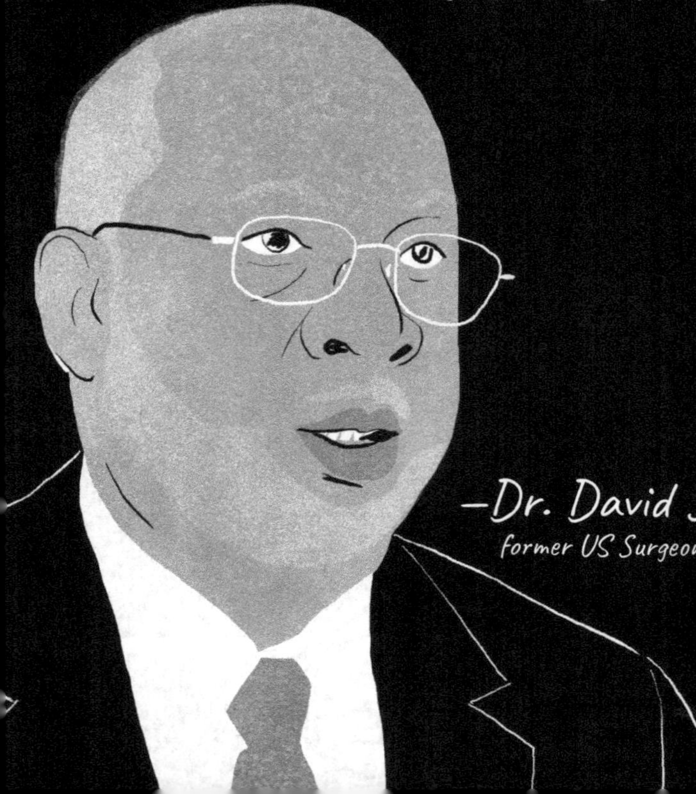

—Dr. David Satcher
former US Surgeon General

2

GUN DEATHS AND TRAUMA

The US vs. the World

The human and financial toll of gun violence in the US is enormous, when we consider the deaths, injuries, trauma, community devastation, and financial costs of this scourge.

FIREARM DEATHS AND INJURIES

- In 2021, 48,830 people died as a result of gunfire. Most of these shootings were intentional firearm assaults and suicides
- There are over 100,000 nonfatal firearm injuries each year
- Unintentional (accidental) firearm deaths account for about 1 percent of all gun deaths
- Firearm deaths now surpass deaths from motor vehicle accidents

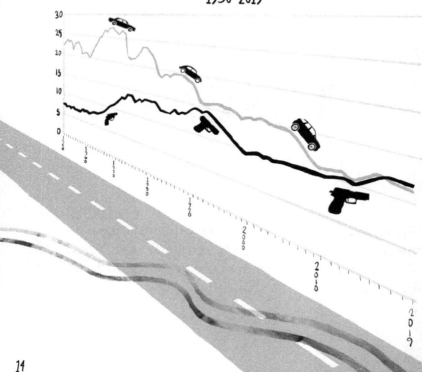

DEATH RATES PER 100,000 PEOPLE BY 🚗 V 🔫
1950-2019

THE US VERSUS THE WORLD

The US has **25 TIMES** the gun homicide rate of other high-income countries combined, when adjusted for population differences.

DATA DATE		NUMBER OF HOMICIDES	ODDS OF BEING SHOT TO DEATH
2014	USA	10,945	1 IN 29,000
2011	ISRAEL	81	1 IN 95,000
2013	CANADA	131	1 IN 271,000
2012	FINLAND	17	1 IN 319,000
2013	SWITZERLAND	18	1 IN 452,000
2013	AUSTRALIA	35	1 IN 655,000
2012	SPAIN	51	1 IN 918,000
2011	GERMANY	61	< 1 IN 1,000,000
2011-12	UK	38	< 1 IN 1,000,000
2008	JAPAN	11	< 1 IN 10,000,000

The leading cause of death for Americans under 20 is gunfire. This cause now surpasses deaths from motor vehicle accidents. Gun deaths for children and teens have spiked *87%* from 2011-2021. In the other countries listed, motor vehicle accidents and cancer are the leading causes of death for this age group and firearms are no higher than #3 top cause of death.

US CHILD DEATH RATES
2021

CAUSE OF CHILD DEATH RANKINGS
2021 (US) – 2019 (OTHER COUNTRIES)

	1	2	3	4	5
US	Firearms	Motor Vehicles	Cancer	Substance Abuse	Heart Disease
AUSTRALIA	Motor Vehicles	Cancer	Heart Disease	Substance Abuse	Firearms
AUSTRIA	Motor Vehicles	Cancer	Substance Abuse	Heart Disease	Firearms
BELGIUM	Motor Vehicles	Cancer	Substance Abuse	Heart Disease	Firearms
CANADA	Motor Vehicles	Cancer	Firearms	Substance Abuse	Heart Disease
FRANCE	Motor Vehicles	Cancer	Heart Disease	Firearms	Substance Abuse
GERMANY	Cancer	Motor Vehicles	Heart Disease	Firearms	Substance Abuse
JAPAN	Cancer	Motor Vehicles	Heart Disease	Substance Abuse	Firearms
NETHERLANDS	Cancer	Motor Vehicles	Heart Disease	Substance Abuse	Firearms
SWEDEN	Cancer	Motor Vehicles	Substance Abuse = Heart Disease	Heart Disease	Firearms
SWITZERLAND	Cancer	Motor Vehicles	Firearms	Substance Abuse = Heart Disease	Heart Disease
UK	Cancer	Motor Vehicles	Heart Disease	Substance Abuse	Firearms

FIREARMS MOTOR VEHICLES CANCER SUBSTANCE ABUSE HEART DISEASE

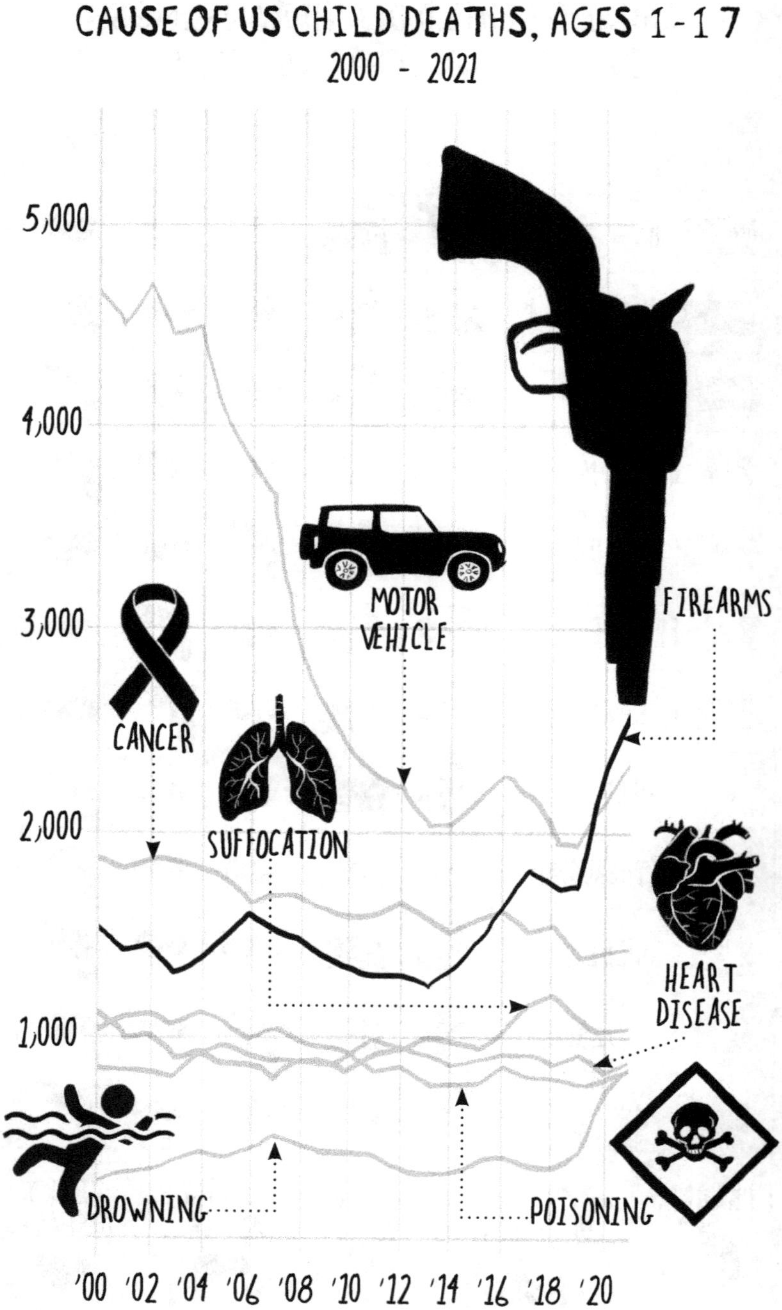

CAUSE OF US CHILD DEATHS, AGES 1-17
2000 - 2021
5,000
4,000
3,000
2,000
1,000
MOTOR VEHICLE
FIREARMS
CANCER
SUFFOCATION
HEART DISEASE
DROWNING
POISONING
'00 '02 '04 '06 '08 '10 '12 '14 '16 '18 '20

MASS SHOOTINGS

In the US, mass shootings about doubled compared to 2014-2018.

In 2023, the US exceeded

600

mass shootings for the fourth consecutive year.

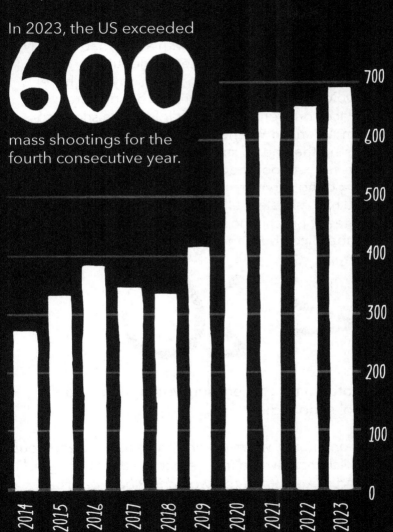

SOCIAL AND EMOTIONAL EFFECTS OF GUN VIOLENCE

- Over half of Americans are personally affected by gun violence, as they have been shot or intimidated by someone with a gun, had a family member shot, or witnessed a shooting
- Close to one in three Americans say they have avoided or have considered avoiding certain places or events due to their fear of a shooting
- An American Psychological Association survey has found that the #1 stressor for teens is the fear of a mass or school shooting
- Shooting survivors under age 20 have substantially higher rates of psychiatric illness and substance abuse than their peers

A quote from a student survivor of the Uvalde school shooting:

> *"Sometimes, when my anxiety makes me zone out, I wish that I would just be back in the fourth grade and wake up and this would just be a bad, bad dream," Daniel told me. "My friends, cousins and I will never be the same again... I miss how happy I used to be. I hate how I can't stop my head from spinning or thinking of things that can go bad."*

Jennifer Guttenberg, mother of 14-year-old Parkland school shooting victim Jaime, read the following victim impact statement in court at the sentencing trial of the shooter. Her statement illustrates the devastating and far-reaching psychological effects of such shootings on the victims' families:

It's impossible to describe life without Jaime in the short amount of time that I have been given here, but I will try my best. Every day I live with the fact that Jaime's life was cut too short and was unable to show the world her fullest potential.

She missed out on a lifetime of things…high school experiences, dance classes with her friends, high school graduation, moving away to college and college graduation, her first job, getting married, and having kids of her own. The list goes on and on.

The pain of this is unbearable. My life feels empty, lonely, and incomplete. There are days that the sadness is so overwhelming, and the crying comes from deep within the gut and causes physical pain. I relive that day over and over in my mind and can't sleep well. I can't get the thoughts and images of what happened out of my head. My career has suffered, as working with other people's children is now so emotionally taxing. My outlook on life has completely changed in such a negative way. It takes strength just to get through each day. One day at a time we say, even many years later. I lost my daughter, my flesh and blood, the baby that grew inside of me and then, in an instant, she was gone. I lost my purpose in life that day.

Alithia Haven Ramirez had just turned 10 years old when she, along with 18 of her classmates and two of her teachers, were shot and killed at Robb Elementary School in Uvalde, Texas. Alithia's parents Jess Hernandez and Ryan Ramirez made short statements as part of a social media campaign created by Violet Lemay, the illustrator of this book.

Jess wrote on social media:

> *I find it increasingly difficult to cope with the loss of my baby girl. The constant reminders of her absence are significantly affecting my mental health, making it excruciating to keep her memory alive when it only reminds me of why she's not by my side. Her absence has left a gaping hole in my heart, and I miss her more with each passing day. I wish I could have done something to prevent her death and have her back in my life.*

FINANCIAL COSTS OF GUN VIOLENCE

The annual cost of gun violence in the US is $557 billion (2.6 percent of the US gross domestic product).

These costs cover:

- Medical treatment of gunshot wounds
- Physical rehabilitation and psychological counseling
- Justice system expenditures for law enforcement, courts, and correctional services
- Violence prevention—security systems and personnel
- Loss of income for victims
- Quality of life costs that place a dollar figure on a person's inability to enjoy a normal life and that are based on jury awards in cases initiated by victims or survivors

"WHY MUST WE RELEARN A LESSON WE CODIFIED CENTURIES AGO?

HOW DUMB ARE WE?"

—Robert Spitzer
political scientist, referring to restrictions on gun carrying dating back to colonial times

GUN LAWS IN AMERICA
A Brief History

It is widely believed that gun restrictions are a recent development and that America's past was marked by gunfights and total lawlessness. This section will show that gun laws, often far stricter than those today, existed from America's earliest days.

EARLY DAYS

As early as 1686, New Jersey prohibited wearing weapons because they were said to induce "great Fear and Quarrels."

During the revolutionary period, states formed militias as America had no standing army. That era was marked by strict gun laws requiring all free men to acquire militarily useful firearms and to attend periodic gatherings (musters), during which the guns were inspected and recorded by officials—an early form of gun registration. In some states (e.g., New Hampshire), officials conducted door-to-door inventories of guns available in the community and the states could seize guns if they were needed for military purposes.

MUSTER ROLLS like this one from Kansas were kept by militia officials, listing each member of the militia, his rank, and details about his firearm.

THE NOT-SO-WILD WEST

Contrary to Hollywood depictions, the Old West had low rates of violence and many gun ordinances prohibited gun carrying in towns and inside bars. Regulation in frontier towns was quite strict. In notorious Dodge City, Kansas, for example, people were required to turn in their guns when they entered the town. Contrary to the mythology of violence-ridden Western towns beset by shootouts, an average of just one to two murders per year occurred in Dodge City during the cattle era. The shootouts depicted in countless books and movies were "unheard of."

THE SOUTH

Gun regulation was also prevalent in the South, a region with some of the most restrictive gun laws in the nineteenth century. These laws were designed to prevent gunfights and to disarm Black people following the Civil War. Laws banning the carrying of concealed weapons were widespread and generally believed to be an essential part of preventing violence.

Alabama's 1839 law banning the carrying of concealed weapons was titled, "An Act to Suppress the Evil Practice of Carrying Weapons Secretly." By the early 1900s, over 40 states outlawed or restricted gun carrying due to rising violence. By contrast, all states currently allow the carrying of concealed firearms.

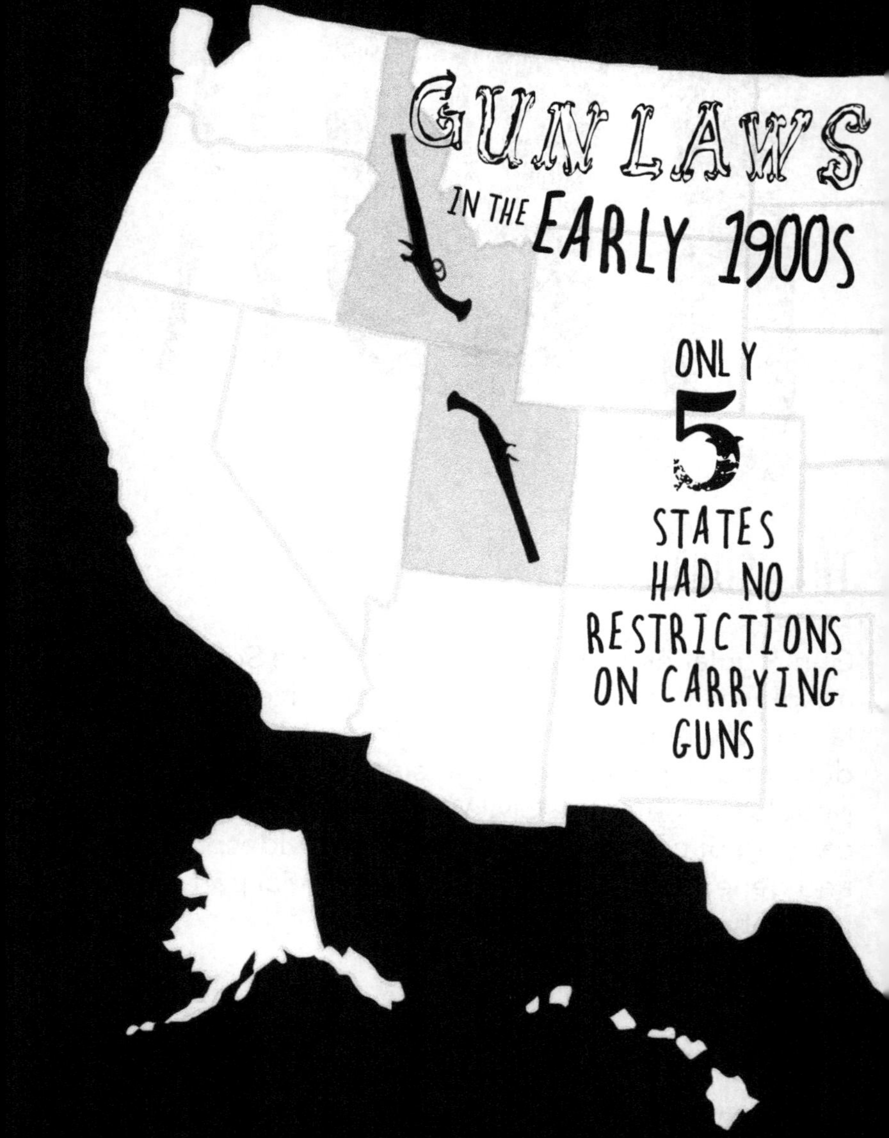
GUN LAWS
IN THE EARLY 1900S
ONLY
5
STATES
HAD NO
RESTRICTIONS
ON CARRYING
GUNS

GUN RESTRICTIONS

NO GUN RESTRICTIONS

90%

OF AMERICA'S STATES AND
TERRITORIES, INCLUDING
WASHINGTON DC,
OUTLAWED OR RESTRICTED
GUN CARRYING DUE TO
RISING VIOLENCE.

TODAY,
ALL STATES ALLOW
THE CARRYING
OF CONCEALED
WEAPONS.

"THIS IS A GUN CULTURE. WE LOVE GUNS."

— Bill Maher
political commentator
and television host

4

GUN CULTURE IN AMERICA

Bill Maher is wrong. While the US has the most armed population, most Americans are not part of any gun culture. Despite poems like "America is a Gun", a relatively small minority has given people around the world the impression that most Americans worship guns.

ARE MOST AMERICANS GUN OWNERS?

America is awash with guns, with about 400 million privately-owned guns in a country of 330 million people, including assault-style weapons designed for the military (e.g., AR-15s). However, the figures show that the majority of guns are in the hands of a minority of citizens.

JUST ONE THIRD of adults personally own a gun.

SUPEROWNERS
6% own two-thirds of the nation's guns.

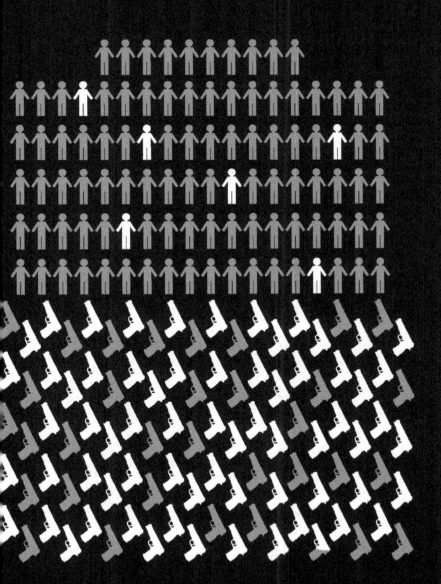

GUN OWNERSHIP VARIES GREATLY
across regions, community size, and states, as well as across age, gender, and racial/ethnic groups.

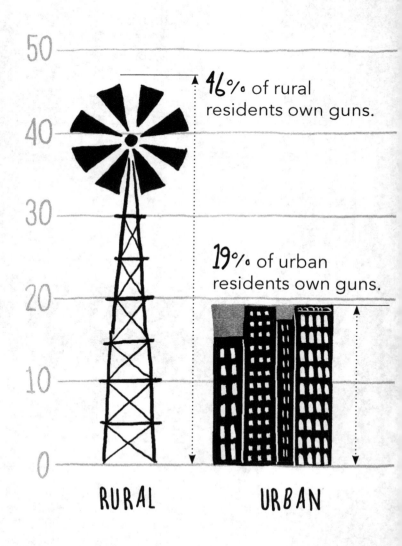

A study covering 2016-2020 found that 13 of the 20 US counties with the most gun homicides per capita were rural and that, in 2020, the total gun death rate per 100,000 was 40 percent higher in rural communities than it was in large metropolitan areas.

PERCENTAGE OF GUN OWNERS BY STATE

Only **8%** of people in **HAWAII** and **NEW JERSEY** own guns.

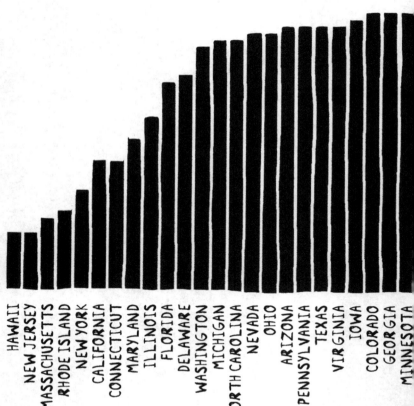

At **64%**, the state with the highest percentage of gun owners is **MONTANA**.

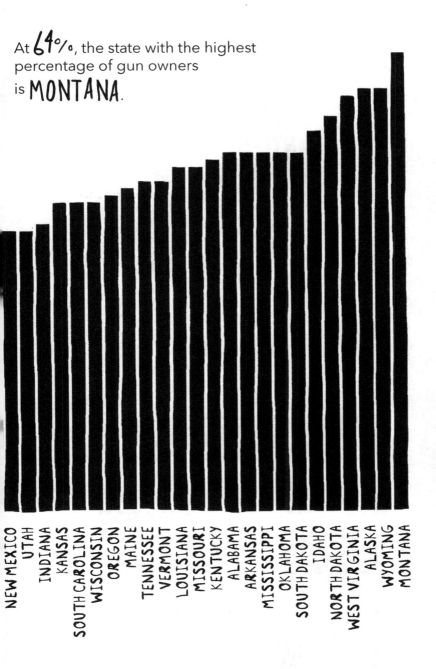

GENDER

39% of men own guns.

22% of women own guns.

RACIAL/ETHNIC GROUPS

36% of WHITES

24% of BLACKS

15% of HISPANICS

...own guns.

RURAL WHITE MALES who are middle-aged or older are the most armed group in the American population.

THE DECLINE OF GUN OWNERSHIP

Despite spikes in gun ownership over the last few decades, the overall trend is clearly heading downward.

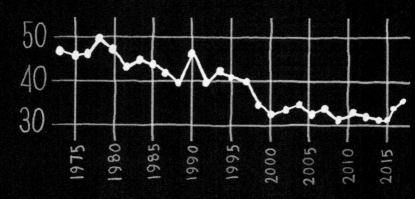

THE DECLINE OF GUNS FOR HUNTING

The proportion of households involved in hunting is half of what it was in the mid-1970s.

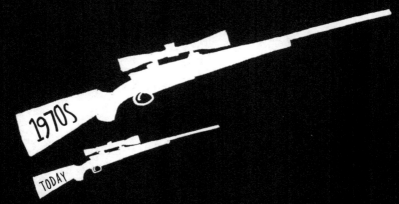

SELF-PROTECTION

Those citing self-protection as the reason for buying a gun rose from 26% in 1999 to 72% in 2023. This trend is significant because guns kept for self-protection are more likely to be kept loaded and accessible than guns kept for hunting, collecting or target shooting.

DAILY CARRY

While increasing noticeably, just 8% of gun owners carry a gun on a daily basis.

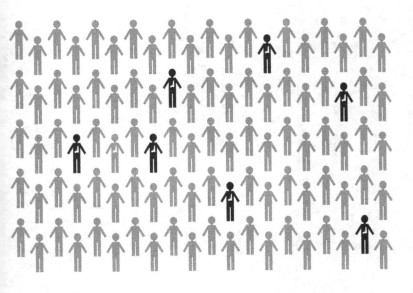

PUBLIC OPINION

More than six times as many Americans say that it is too easy to legally buy a gun as those who say it is too hard to buy a gun. Even many gun owners agree with this statement.

Six in 10 Americans favor stricter gun laws and just a small minority favor more relaxed laws.

STRICTER

JUST RIGHT

MORE RELAXED

"I KEEP HEARING THIS #@!*ING THING THAT GUNS DON'T KILL PEOPLE, BUT PEOPLE KILL PEOPLE.

IF THAT'S THE CASE, WHY DO WE GIVE PEOPLE GUNS WHEN THEY GO TO WAR? WHY NOT JUST SEND THE PEOPLE?"

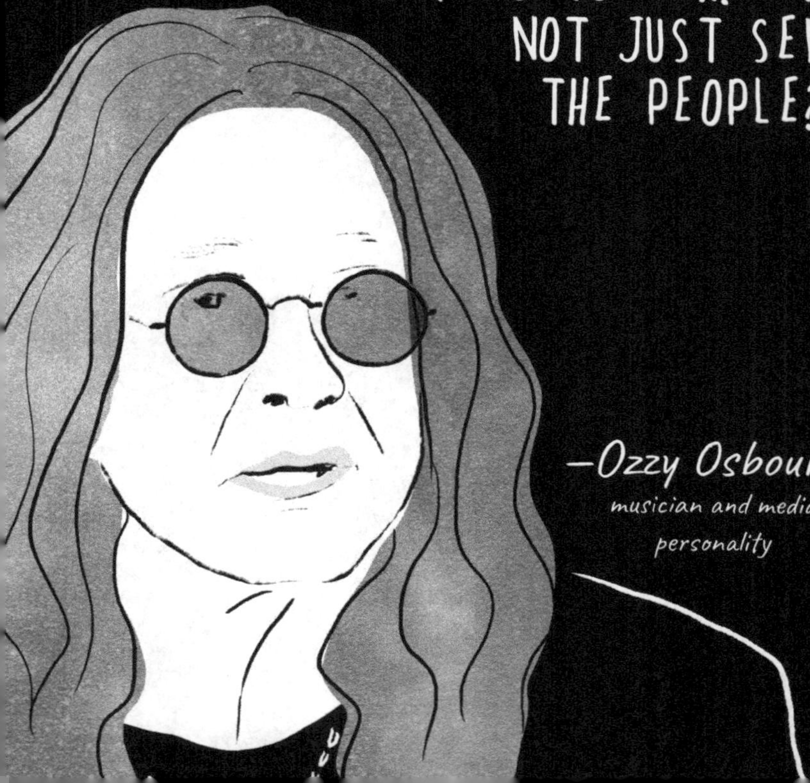

—*Ozzy Osbourne*

musician and media personality

5

GUNS DO KILL
The Weapon Matters

We often hear the slogan: "Guns don't kill, people do." Guns are portrayed as simple inanimate objects; therefore it is argued that the shooter's intent rather than the weapon explains violence. But tools matter in violence as they do to a carpenter or surgeon. Cars and planes are inanimate objects but they help us transport people and freight. Guns help us kill.

WHAT EMERGENCY ROOM DOCTORS AND TRAUMA SURGEONS SAY

To illustrate that guns influence the seriousness of injuries independent of the intent of an aggressor or suicidal individual, consider the laws of physics and how they apply to the danger posed by a firearm. If various features of a gun or ammunition make them more lethal, then it follows that a gun, which can fire bullets at thousands of feet per second, will be more lethal than a knife being wielded by a person at just a few feet per second.

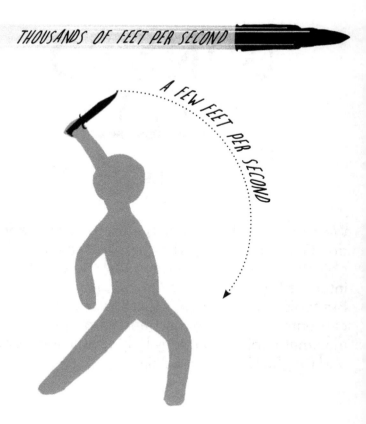

Dr. Arthur Kellermann, a renowned emergency room physician and gun violence researcher, made the following observations on the factors that make guns and ammunition more or less lethal:

> *The specific capacity of a firearm to cause injury depends on its accuracy, the rate of fire, muzzle velocity, and specific characteristics of the projectile [bullet]… Weapons with high muzzle velocities, e.g., hunting rifles, generally cause greater tissue damage than weapons with lower muzzle velocities, e.g., handguns. However, the size, shape, and nature of the projectile also play a powerful role in determining the severity of the resultant injury… A slower bullet, designed to mushroom or fragment on impact, may damage a much larger amount of tissue through direct trauma, cavitation, and shock wave effects… Damage also increases in direct proportion to the mass of the projectile. The number of projectiles striking the body also influences the expected severity of injury.*

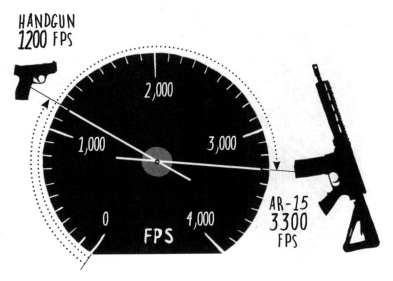

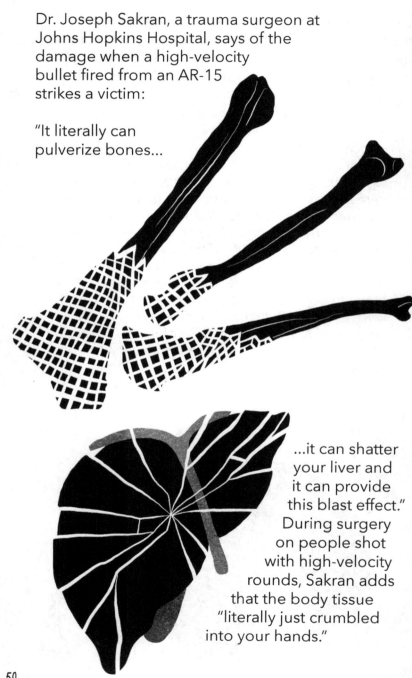

Dr. Joseph Sakran, a trauma surgeon at Johns Hopkins Hospital, says of the damage when a high-velocity bullet fired from an AR-15 strikes a victim:

"It literally can pulverize bones...

...it can shatter your liver and it can provide this blast effect." During surgery on people shot with high-velocity rounds, Sakran adds that the body tissue "literally just crumbled into your hands."

CRIMES: GUNS VERSUS OTHER WEAPONS

A large study of robberies (including holdups and muggings) at Duke University found a strong link between the weapon used and the likelihood of a fatal outcome.

ODDS OF MURDER DURING ROBBERY

AT GUNPOINT
1 IN 250

NO WEAPON
1 IN 5,000

AT KNIFEPOINT
1 IN 750

A study using Chicago Police data found that assaults with firearms were five times as likely to result in the victim's death as knife attacks. The study showed that the difference in lethality was due to the weapon and not different intent of gun and knife attackers.

A POLICE CHIEF SPEAKS OUT

On August 4, 2019, 35 people were shot in under 30 seconds in Dayton, Ohio's Oregon entertainment district. The shooter used an AR-15 style rifle equipped with a drum magazine holding 100 rounds of ammunition. Police officers patrolling the district responded within minutes but it was not soon enough. Dayton's police chief, Richard Biehl, had the following to say about the futility of the rapid response by his officers:

> *Despite their best efforts, their heroic efforts, their extraordinarily rapid response to this horrific threat… and still nine dead and 20 others injured… It's amazing the harm a person can cause in such an extraordinarily short period of time when they have a high-velocity weapon with an enormous amount of ammunition… There's a balance between protecting oneself and providing weapons and equipment that allows mass shootings to occur and for victims to be injured or killed at a rate of more than one per second… That's unconscionable and that's something that can't be deemed reasonable.*

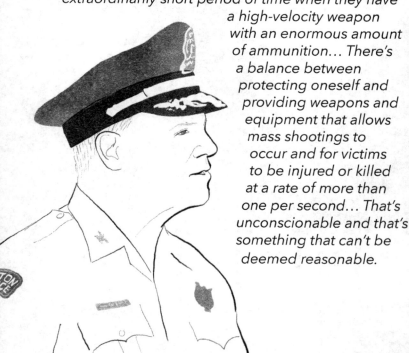

POLITICAL ASSASSINATIONS AND KILLINGS OF POLICE USUALLY INVOLVE FIREARMS

All American presidential assassinations have involved firearms.

Police officers are almost always killed with a gun when they are the targets of homicide. In 2021, of law enforcement officers killed on duty, 61 were shot, whereas four were beaten and three were stabbed to death.

"CIVILIAN SALES WERE NEVER THE INTENDED PURPOSE OF THE AR-15."

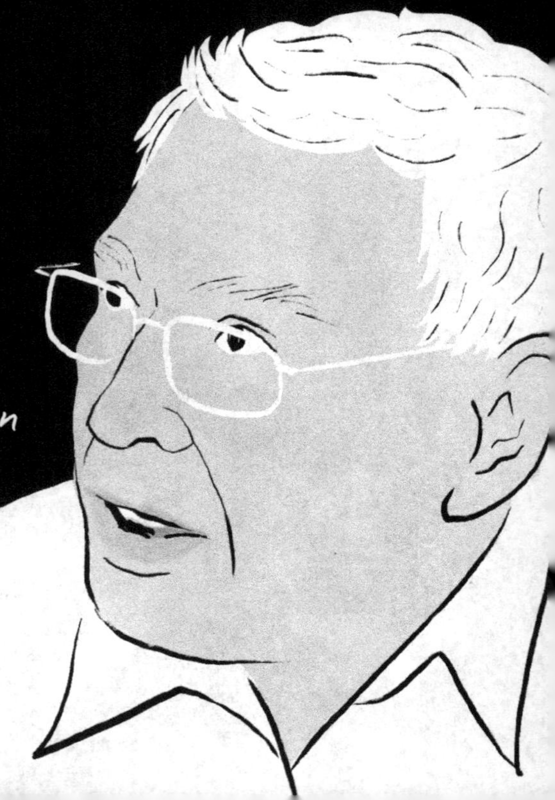

—*Jim Sullivan*
co-designer of the AR-15

6

LETHALITY OF TODAY'S WEAPONS

Today's weapons are far more lethal than those available to civilians 40 to 50 years ago and beyond anything imagined by the Framers who drafted the Second Amendment. The development of weapons like the AR-15 is increasing the frequency and lethality of mass shootings despite medical advances that would normally reduce the carnage.

THE AR-15 WAS DESIGNED FOR THE MILITARY, NOT FOR SPORT

Faced with the recurring threat of another federal assault weapons ban, the gun lobby and industry began to refer to guns like the AR-15 as a "sporting gun." ArmaLite, Inc. first developed the AR-15 in the 1950s as a lightweight military rifle but sold the design to Colt after they had little success selling it. In the 1960s, the US military selected Colt to manufacture the automatic rifle (machine gun) used by US troops in Vietnam. This rifle, based on the design for the AR-15, was known as the M-16. Following that success, Colt ramped up production of a semiautomatic version of the M-16 for law enforcement and the public, marketing it as the AR-15. When Colt's patents for the AR-15 expired in the 1970s, other gunmakers created similar models. AR-15 is now the generic term for these firearms.

"Now You Can Buy a Hot Combat Rifle for Sport"

Popular Science 1965

Jim Sullivan helped design the AR-15. Responding to questions about the role of these firearms in a civilian context, he stated: "Of course, everybody gets concerned when there's one of these school issues where children are killed by an AR-15. I mean, that's sickening. But that was never the intended purpose. Civilian sales were never the intended purpose."

The principal designer of the AR-15 was Eugene Stoner, an ex-Marine who initially designed rifles in his garage. Cameron McWhirter and Zusha Elinson, national reporters for the Wall Street Journal and authors of the definitive book detailing the history of the AR-15, write that Stoner "sought to design a lightweight, easy-to-use weapon for US troops and their allies during the Cold War." General Wyman of the US Army was impressed with one of Stoner's earlier models—the AR-10—and was seeking a rifle that weighed six pounds fully loaded with a 20-round magazine that fired small-caliber bullets. He also required that the bullets should have enough power to penetrate a steel helmet at a distance of 500 yards. These requirements were met by Stoner in the AR-15.

"The Sporter looks like, feels like, and performs like its military cousin."

Colt Firearms 1977

THE AR-15 VERSUS REVOLUTIONARY ERA FIREARMS

There is much controversy about the US Constitution's Second Amendment which refers to the "right to keep and bear arms"(see more in Chapter 11). To gain insight into whether the Framers of the Constitution meant that millions of

BROWN BESS REVOLUTIONARY WAR MUSKET

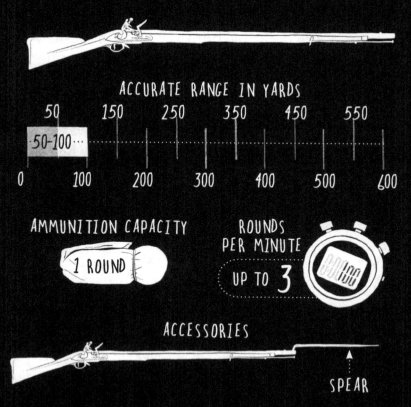

civilians could possess weapons like the AR-15, let's examine the musket, the most common type of firearm in the late 1700s. Muskets were slow to load, as they were muzzle-loaded, meaning the powder and bullet were poured into the barrel. They needed to be loaded after every shot. It took about 30 seconds to load a musket. Experienced shooters could fire three shots in a minute.

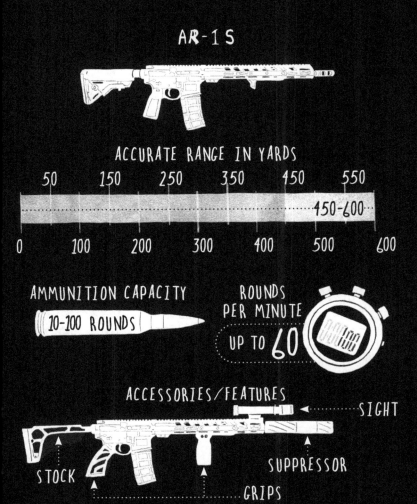

MASSACRES INVOLVING THE AR-15 STYLE RIFLES

All of the top 10 deadliest mass shootings since 2010 were committed with assault rifles like the AR-10 and AR-15.

Year	Location	Site	DEATHS	INJURIES
2017	LAS VEGAS NEVADA	LAS VEGAS STRIP	58	867
2016	ORLANDO FLORIDA	PULSE NIGHTCLUB	49	58
2012	NEWTON CONNECTICUT	SANDY HOOK ELEMENTARY	27	2
2017	SUTHERLAND SPRINGS TEXAS	FIRST BAPTIST CHURCH	26	22
2019	EL PASO TEXAS	WALMART	23	23
2022	UVALDE TEXAS	ROBB ELEMENTARY SCHOOL	21	15
2023	LEWISTON MAINE	BOWLING ALLEY & RESTAURANT	18	13
2018	PARKLAND FLORIDA	MARJORY STONEMAN DOUGLAS H.S.	17	17
2015	SAN BERNADINO CALIFORNIA	INLAND REGIONAL CENTER	14	24
2012	AURORA COLORADO	CENTURY 16 MOVIE THEATER	12	70

SCENES OF CARNAGE WHEN ASSAULT WEAPONS USED

The velocity at which rounds leave an AR-15 style rifle, their range (about 500 yards), rate of fire (frequently resulting in multiple bullet wounds to the victim), and ability to receive very large ammunition magazines all contribute to the lethality of these weapons and the carnage they can produce.

We did not include actual crime scene photos, but the drawing below provides an idea of the carnage that results when AR-15 style weapons are used to maximize casualties. The drawing reflects crime scenes in crowded places that have experienced a mass shooting.

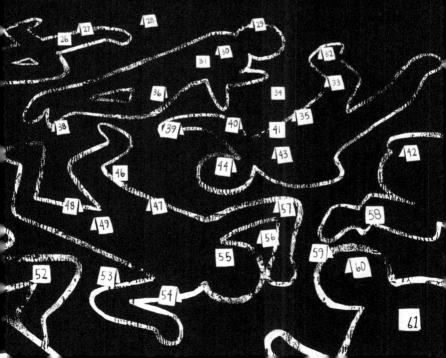

AR-15'S UNIQUE FEATURES

Mike Weisser, a former gun dealer, firearm trainer, and author, states that the US is the only advanced country that fails to restrict weapons of war like the AR-15 style rifles.

Weisser adds:
> *Both the military and civilian versions of the assault gun have a radically different internal design which creates a much quicker movement of the bolt and therefore means that the semi-auto delivery of each round is much faster… The kid who murdered 26 adults and children at the Sandy Hook Elementary School using an AR-15 needed less than three minutes of firing time to blast out more than 90 rounds. Additionally, not only does the gun load from the bottom of the frame, which allows the shooter to use a magazine of almost unlimited size and capacity, but the mechanism which releases an empty magazine and locks in a loaded magazine also operates much more quickly than other bottom-loading guns. Taken together, these design features, as well as the light weight of the gun which makes it more maneuverable in small spaces like a small room or hallway, makes the so-called "modern sporting gun" as lethal as any gun could be.*

HIGH CALIBER HANDGUNS

It's not just rifles that have become so much more lethal from the time the Constitution's Second Amendment was drafted. In the 1980s and early 1990s, there was a rapid shift in handguns from revolvers to semiautomatic pistols and to larger caliber weapons. Revolvers typically had six rounds of ammunition, whereas pistols today, like the Glock 17, can have 17 rounds in the magazine and one in the chamber. Semiautomatic pistols also fire faster. Victims of gun assaults today typically have more bullet wounds than they did in the 1980s and higher caliber handguns are deadlier.

A Boston study demonstrates the greater lethality of high caliber handguns.

INCREASED ODDS OF DEATH FROM SHOOTING

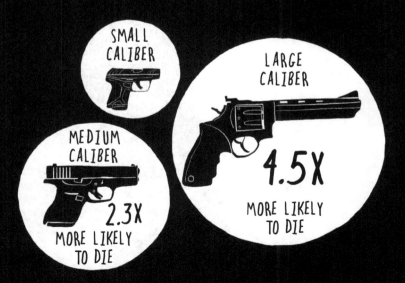

"THE ONLY THING THAT STOPS A BAD GUY WITH A GUN IS A **GOOD GUY WITH A GUN.**"

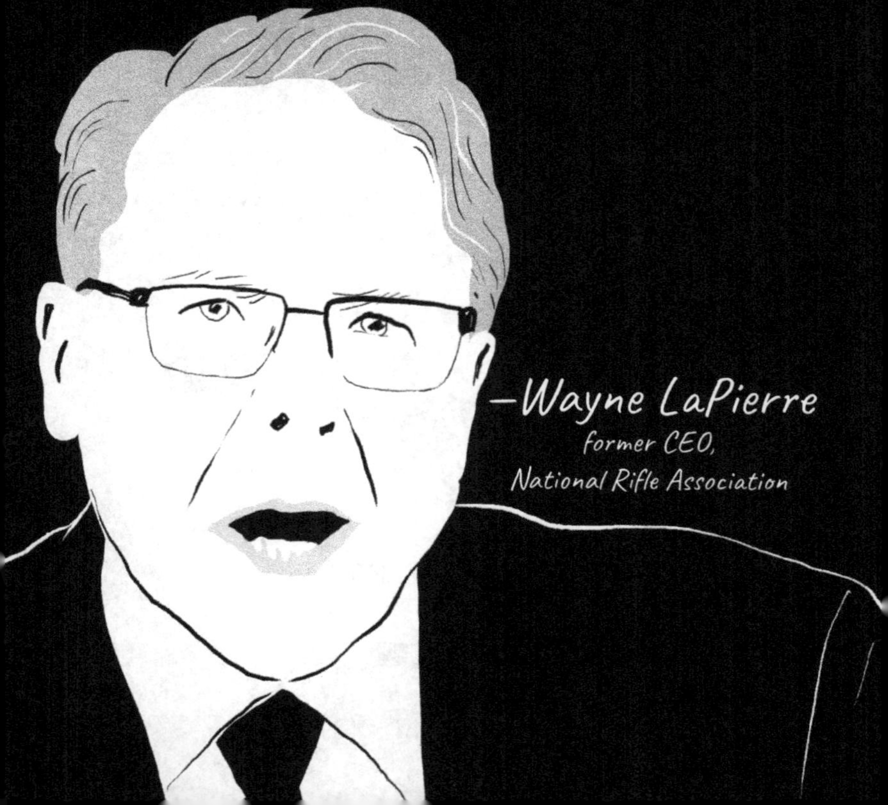

—*Wayne LaPierre*
former CEO,
National Rifle Association

SELF-DEFENSE
Reality or Illusion?

Following the horrific Sandy Hook mass shooting in Connecticut that killed 20 elementary school students and six adults, many expected even the most ardent gun rights advocates to agree that unstable individuals like the shooter should never get their hands on a gun, especially one designed for combat. Instead, Wayne LaPierre of the National Rifle Association, doubling down on gun rights, stated: "The only thing that stops a bad guy with a gun is a good guy with a gun."

EXAGGERATED CLAIMS OF DEFENSIVE GUN USES

Armed self-defense advocates often refer to a survey conducted by criminologists Gary Kleck and Mark Gertz in the 1990s purporting to show that there are as many as 2.5 million annual uses of guns for self-defense in the US. At that time, there were fewer than a million annual criminal uses of guns. How can there be 1.5 million more defensive than criminal uses of a gun unless we consider using a gun against an unarmed individual a legitimate defensive use?

Serious Problems with Kleck & Gertz's Claims:
- The study relied on 150 survey respondents to derive estimates for the entire country
- Kleck/Gertz made no attempt to assess whether respondents' actions were truly defensive
- In just a fifth of the cases was the respondent actually attacked
- Most of the adversaries were not armed
- Kleck/Gertz acknowledge that their national estimates would have been 340,000-400,000 if only cases in which respondents' lives were in serious danger were considered
- The study claimed 845,000 annual defensive gun uses during burglaries, a number that exceeds all burglaries in which residents had a gun, were home, and were awake

A number of researchers nominate the Kleck and Gertz findings as "the most outrageous number mentioned in a policy discussion."

Criminal court judges evaluated reported self-defense uses of guns by participants in two Harvard University surveys. In over half the cases, the majority of judges rated the purported self-defense actions as "probably illegal."

THE NATIONAL CRIME VICTIMIZATION SURVEY

This is the largest and most credible annual survey of criminal victimizations involving interviews with persons from 150,000 households. A study of 14,000 personal "contact" crimes from the 2007-2011 national surveys found that a gun was used in self-defense in fewer than 1 percent of the cases.

Overall, for the years 2007-2011, national survey respondents reported about half a million firearm-related victimizations a year and fewer than 50,000 defensive gun uses per year—10 criminal gun uses for every defensive gun use.

JUSTIFIABLE HOMICIDES

While all criminal justice statistics are subject to some error due to underreporting of crime and other reasons, homicide statistics are the most reliable as most homicides are reported and are investigated more rigorously.

In 2019, FBI data showed that there were 10,258 reported firearm homicides and just 334 justifiable homicides with firearms. For every self-defense killing with a gun, there were 31 criminal homicides with guns, showing that guns are many times more likely to be used to commit murders than to kill in self-defense.

SELF-DEFENSE KILLING

CRIMINAL HOMICIDES

DR. KELLERMANN'S RESEARCH ON GUNS IN THE HOME

Dr. Arthur Kellermann, an emergency room physician and epidemiologist, has been one of the most influential gun violence researchers. His studies consistently show that guns in the home pose a risk of violence to the occupants.

Kellermann and his colleagues studied over 400 homicides occurring in residences in three counties. They found that when homes were matched on factors like neighborhood, race, age, violence in the home, and illegal drug use, homes with guns were almost three times as likely to experience a homicide as homes without guns.

In another study led by Dr. Kellermann, for every legally justifiable self-defense shooting with a gun kept in the home, there were 22 firearm-related assaults or murders, suicide attempts, or accidental shootings in or around the residence. This study shows clearly that guns in the home are far more likely to harm members of the household than to be used against an intruder.

ARMED CITIZENS RARELY THWART SHOOTERS AND CAN CONFUSE POLICE

Studies of active shooter incidents show that armed citizens rarely intervene to stop the shooter. An FBI study of 333 of these incidents, defined as one in which an individual is actively engaged in killing or attempting to kill people in a confined area, found that in just four (1 percent) of these incidents was a suspect killed by an armed civilian.

In another incident occurring on July 7, 2016, an individual opened fire and killed five Dallas police officers. The officers were on duty to provide security at a demonstration where the killing of African American men was being protested. About 20 to 30 open-carry activists were also on the scene, carrying assault weapons and wearing fatigues and body armor. Police Chief Brown stated that the armed individuals impeded the law enforcement response by creating confusion as to who the shooter was and whether there were multiple shooters.

Dallas' Chief Brown stated:

> We're trying as best we can as a law enforcement community to make it work so that citizens can express their Second Amendment rights. But it's increasingly challenging when people have AR-15s slung over their shoulder and they're in a crowd. We don't know who the good guy is versus the bad guy when everyone starts shooting.

THE EFFECTS OF RIGHT-TO-CARRY LAWS

Beginning in the 1980s, the gun lobby and its allies campaigned to allow residents of all states to carry firearms. They argued that Americans would be much safer with such a policy. The evidence indicates the opposite.

Professor John Donohue and his colleagues have found that state right-to-carry laws are associated with a 13 to 15 percent increase in violent crime 10 years after their enactment. These laws therefore increase violence rather than serve as a deterrent to crime.

In addition, people do not feel safer with more gun carrying in their communities. A Harvard University survey found that five times as many Americans said they would feel less safe, as opposed to safer, if they learned that more of their neighbors were carrying guns.

SAFER

LESS SAFE

SIDE EFFECTS OF GUN CARRYING

When we examine gun carrying, we must also look at the downsides so people can weigh the costs as well as potential benefits of carrying lethal weapons. Carrying guns can escalate the seriousness of spontaneous arguments or disputes. There are accidental discharges where people are shot unintentionally, and guns left in cars can be stolen and used in crime.

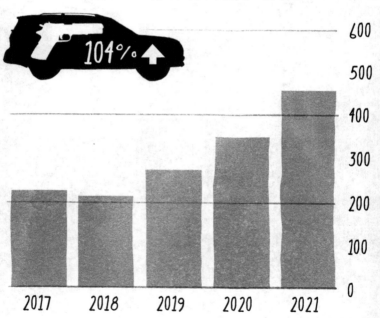

With surging gun carrying in recent years, road rage shootings have doubled nationally from 2017 to 2021. Such incidents cannot occur unless people carry firearms, and the daily carrying of guns is increasing in the US.

STAND YOUR GROUND LAWS

Most states have some version of a Stand Your Ground (SYG) law. These laws give individuals the right to use deadly force when they have a "reasonable belief" that they are facing death or serious injury. Traditionally, self-defense laws allowed for the use of lethal force when no other action was available that would allow the person to survive. An individual who was able to "talk down" an attacker or leave the scene could not lawfully use lethal force to thwart the attacker. This is referred to as the "duty to retreat." SYG laws remove this duty to retreat, allowing a person facing a threat to move directly to lethal force even though they could have de-escalated a confrontation.

Florida's SYG law was associated with a 32 percent increase in firearm-related homicides. It is estimated that an additional 4,200 people were murdered with a gun in Florida in the 10-year period following enactment of SYG.

32%

Homicide rates in 21 states with a SYG law increased by an average of 8 percent over other states, causing 600 more homicides per year in those states alone. Rather than a deterrent, SYG increases violence.

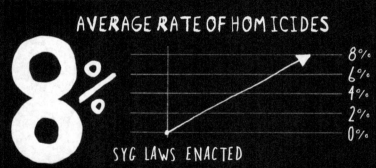

AVERAGE RATE OF HOMICIDES

8%

SYG LAWS ENACTED

Racial disparities are magnified in SYG states. Although racial disparities are also found in states without SYG laws, these disparities were significantly greater in SYG states. In these states, a white shooter who killed a Black victim was

350%

more likely to be found to be justified in the killing than if the same shooter killed a white victim.

TRAINING REQUIRED TO USE A GUN EFFECTIVELY

Over half the states and counting no longer require those wishing to carry a gun to obtain a permit and basic training in the safe handling of a firearm, marksmanship, and in the appropriate (lawful) use of lethal force. Permitless carry laws have been found to increase gun homicides by 22 percent.

Joseph Vince, a former agent with the Bureau of Alcohol, Tobacco, Firearms and Explosives for 27 years, and his associates make the following case for training:

Since a firearm has immense lethality, the act of carrying one cannot be taken lightly. It should be given to those who have demonstrated good judgment, as well as mastered the necessary skills to handle this awesome responsibility. Legislators need to strengthen the vetting process of persons who are authorized to carry a firearm outside a residence. A simple criminal record check is not sufficient. Preventing criminal or accidental tragedies with firearms begins by allowing only those who have been properly trained initially and ongoing —and are known to be nonviolent law-abiding citizens to carry in public. Likewise, no one who has anger, mental, or drug/alcohol issues should be permitted to carry a firearm.

Vince and his associates found that training should include mental preparation, knowledge of the law, and development of situational judgment, as well as expertise, skill, and familiarity with firearms. They recommend basic initial training to receive a permit and biannual recertification. Training should consist of decision-making during real-life scenarios, shooting accuracy in stressful situations, and firing range practice. They add:

> *The average violent attack is over in 3 seconds. They are "blitz" attacks, designed to blindside and overwhelm us. We must be able to comprehend what's happening, orient ourselves to that attack, draw, and begin fighting back within that 3 second window, or else there's a very good chance we'll be defeated before we have a chance to even draw our weapons... And without specific training, many (if not most) of us are prone to freezing for 3 or more seconds when confronted with a sudden, psychologically and physically overwhelming attack.*

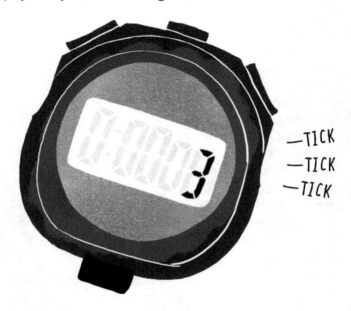

Several studies show that, in combat situations, even trained officers miss the mark more than 80 percent of the time. One training exercise is called the Tueller drill, which requires an armed individual to pull, draw, point a pistol at a nine-inch diameter target which is 21 feet away and get off two shots within two seconds or less. This is based on experience that an aggressor usually reaches the victim within two seconds of the latter having recognized he is being attacked by an armed individual.

Mike Weisser, a former gun dealer and trainer, states that just five percent of his civilian students can successfully complete the Tueller drill after taking his safety course. This result is with a stationary target and without the stress of a combat situation! Imagine the accuracy rate of civilians carrying guns in states requiring no permits or training whatsoever!

“MOST MASS SHOOTINGS ARISE FROM ARGUMENTS BETWEEN INDIVIDUALS OR SMALL GROUPS. THE MAJORITY DO NOT INVOLVE DISTURBED PEOPLE RANDOMLY SELECTING VICTIMS.”

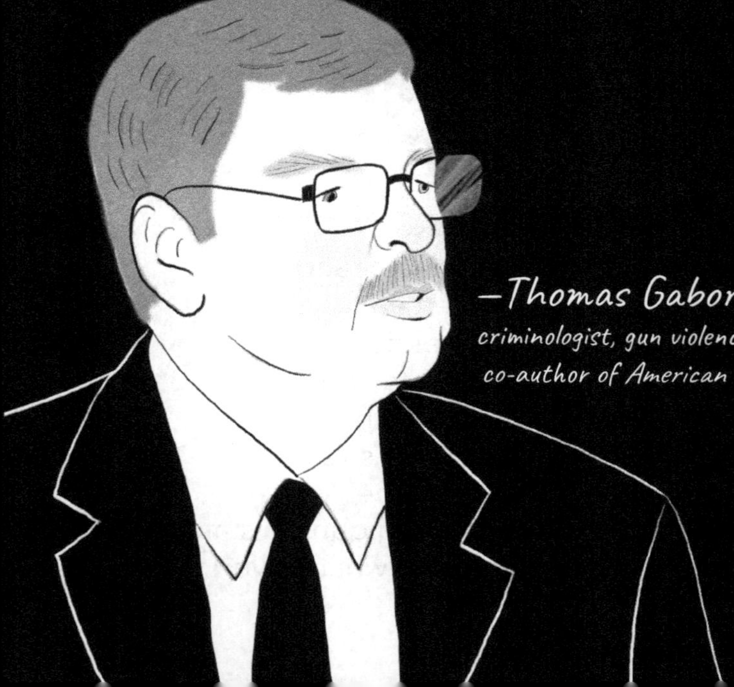

—*Thomas Gabor, PhD*
criminologist, gun violence expert, co-author of American Carnage

8

MASS SHOOTINGS
Random, Targeted, or Reckless?

The public's view of a mass shooting is of a disturbed individual who randomly attacks as many people as possible at a mall, movie theater, school, or other crowded space. Mass shootings are more often due to disputes and some are spontaneous in nature. It is in these spontaneous shootings that weapon carrying makes the greatest difference as the presence of firearms can escalate disputes into homicides. Innocent bystanders are often also killed when shootouts occur or a person fires at another in a crowded place.

TRENDS IN MASS SHOOTINGS

The Gun Violence Archive defines a mass shooting as one in which four or more people, excluding the shooter, are shot—not necessarily killed—at one general time and location. Trends in recent years show that the annual number of mass shootings has about doubled over the last decade.

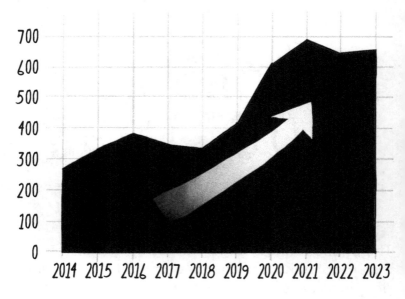

VARIETIES OF MASS SHOOTINGS

There is a wide variety of mass shootings. Most do not fit the popular image of a disturbed individual gunning down as many people, all strangers, as possible. These random shootings make up a small fraction of all incidents. All of the following incidents happened. There is no one profile of a mass shooter or of a shooting. The only common theme is access to firearms and, often, military-grade firearms.

- A shooter enters a movie theater and begins to randomly fire at those in the audience
- A white supremacist enters a supermarket attended mostly by Black people and indiscriminately starts shooting customers
- A man who was just fired returns to his workplace and shoots employees there
- A gang-related shooting takes place outside a club
- A dispute at a house party leads to gunfire by several people
- A man murders family members and commits suicide
- An Air Force aviation student shoots members of the US Navy at a naval station in a terrorist attack

A common form of mass shooting in the US involves a dispute that originates or escalates at a party, club, or park and innocent people are shot due to the recklessness of the shooters. The shooting at the Kansas City Super Bowl parade is a case in point.

Over two dozen people were shot—one person was killed—at the end of the parade. The *New York Times* reports:

> *On the day of the shooting, Mr. Miller and Mr. Mays began arguing as the rally dispersed, a dispute that quickly escalated when both men pulled out guns and began firing at each other, the authorities said... As the argument unfolded, Mr. Young pulled out a gun, advanced toward at least one person and fired several times, the authorities said.*

GUN-FREE ZONES AND MASS SHOOTINGS

Gun rights advocates often argue that mass shootings occur mostly in gun-free zones as there are no armed civilians there to deter a would-be shooter from committing a mass shooting. However, many schools, airports and other venues that do not allow armed civilians still have armed security personnel. Also, many targets are selected because the shooter has a grievance against an employer, family member, a school, a group/gang, or a specific person and not because the location has no armed individuals. There are also many impulsive mass shootings at social events due to an argument that erupts spontaneously and where there is no consideration in advance as to whether the setting is gun-free. Research shows that few shootings occur in true gun-free zones.

In his book *Rampage Nation*, Louis Klarevas found that of 111 gun massacres (six or more victims are killed) 90 percent did not occur in true gun-free zones—zones in which no armed security personnel are stationed and private citizens are prohibited from being armed.

In his book *CARNAGE*, Tom Gabor studied all 1,029 mass shootings committed in the US in 2019 and 2020. He found that a large majority of shootings occurred in locations where guns are allowed, such as residences, streets, apartment complex grounds, businesses, and parking lots. Incidents occurring on the street, in/around residences, and around apartment complexes alone accounted for 63 percent of all mass shootings.

THE CONTAGION EFFECT

Contagion is the idea that one shooting may beget another due to intensive media and social media coverage. Contagion has been observed in the case of suicides and airline hijackings. Some mass shooters are thought to be suicidal and individuals at risk of suicide may be influenced by the suicide of a high-profile individual or by suicides in their environment. After actor Robin Williams took his own life, researchers documented a ten percent surge in suicides in the months following his death.

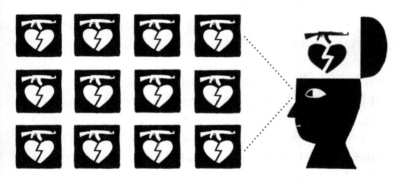

Saturated media coverage often follows high-casualty mass shootings. This coverage tends to repeatedly describe the event in detail, weapons used, the shooter, his ideology (where relevant), and his life story. This detailed coverage can directly influence imitation. The shooter achieves social status through the notoriety gained from the numerous news reports. Images displaying shooters aiming or brandishing guns at the camera project danger and toughness. Individuals may identify with the life story of perpetrators. Repeated reports of body counts reward the act by underscoring the competence of the shooter.

Some shooters have had an obsession with mass shootings or their perpetrators.

- The young man who committed the atrocity at Sandy Hook Elementary School in Newtown, Conn., had studied the Columbine massacre as well as others.
- The individual who shot over 100 people at the Pulse night club in Orlando, Fla., studied a previous attack in San Bernardino, Cal., which was also inspired by a radical Islamic ideology.
- The white nationalist who murdered 23 people in El Paso, Tex., had seen the video posted by the man who committed the mosque massacres in Christchurch, New Zealand.

While not all studies have found evidence that mass shootings spread like a virus, a 2015 study by Sherry Towers and her colleagues does provide evidence that is compelling. They found that that mass shootings were temporarily contagious and increased the probability of future shootings for up to 13 days, with each mass shooting inciting on average 30 percent more attacks.

Following high-profile mass shootings, there is intensive media coverage and social media activity. Survivors and witnesses post news of the event and its aftermath on Facebook, Instagram, Twitter (now X), etc. There are also online communities that treat shooters as heroes and obsess about their habits and actions. Such coverage of shootings and perpetrators provides fertile soil for those who may be inclined to follow in a shooter's footsteps.

Within two weeks of the Parkland (Florida) school shooting, 638 copycat threats targeted schools nationwide.

California experienced four mass shootings in eight days in January 2023. Two of the incidents targeted mostly people of Asian descent. Such a clustering of shootings in a short time span is suggestive, but not proof, of contagion.

The Buffalo (New York) supermarket shooting and Uvalde (Texas) school shooting occurred in May 2022. 17 mass shootings occurred in the 10 days between the two shootings.

8 DAYS

"...A GUN IS NOT, AS SOME WOMEN FANTASIZE, AN EASY EQUALIZER."

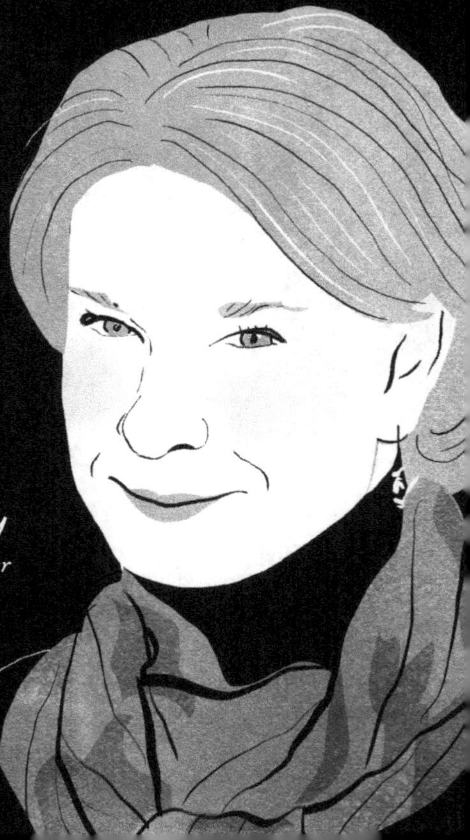

—Caitlin Kelly
writer & handgun owner

9

DO GUNS MAKE WOMEN SAFER?

Advocates for arming women believe that guns are a great equalizer and will protect women from attacks. However, most violence against women is committed in private by male partners rather than in public spaces by strangers. Over nine in 10 women who are murdered are killed by men they know, and most murdered women have been killed with guns. As much violence against women is committed by intimate partners, guns kept by women in the home may be used against them.

GUNS ARE A THREAT TO WOMEN

One study found that women living with a gun in the home are three times more likely to be murdered than women with no guns in the home.

A homicide is eight times more likely to occur when an abuser has access to a firearm.

Abusive partners also threaten and intimidate with a gun. The trauma experienced by women who have been abused is more severe when gun-related threats have been part of the abuse.

SELF-DEFENSE USES OF GUNS BY WOMEN

While some American women are harmed by men wielding guns, it is important to explore the frequency with which women use their guns to protect themselves from harm.

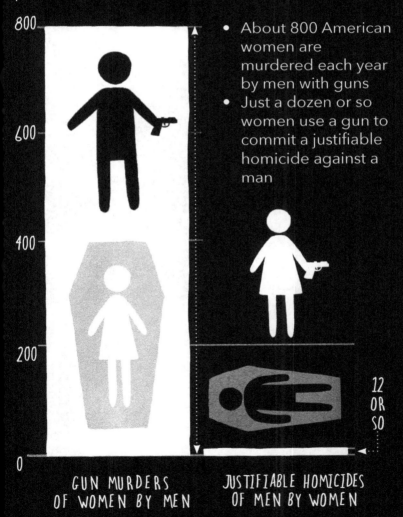

- About 800 American women are murdered each year by men with guns
- Just a dozen or so women use a gun to commit a justifiable homicide against a man

GUN MURDERS OF WOMEN BY MEN

JUSTIFIABLE HOMICIDES OF MEN BY WOMEN

WOMEN SPEAK OUT ABOUT THE DANGERS OF GUN OWNERSHIP

Christy Salters Martin is a former professional boxer and has been a concealed carry permit holder. When she attempted to leave her husband, she was shot with her own gun. She now cautions other women about the perils of gun ownership.

Just putting a weapon in the woman's hand is not going to reduce the number of fatalities or gunshot victims that we have. Too many times, their male counterpart or spouse will be able to overpower them and take that gun away.

Caitlin Kelly, an award-winning freelance writer and handgun owner herself, writes of the responsibility and perils of firearm ownership:

> But a gun is not, as some women fantasize, an easy equalizer... You must only point a loaded gun at someone or something you are fully prepared to destroy, and once you have pointed the barrel, you must be ready and able to squeeze the trigger as many times as necessary. If you truly feel yourself incapable of ever doing so, even to prevent your own death or severe injury, do not buy a gun primarily for self-defense. You are far more likely to be injured or killed with your own weapon if you hesitate, misfire, or fire a few rounds wildly in the hope of merely wounding.

Despite aggressive efforts on the part of the gun industry to market guns to women, the vast majority of women are not interested in owning and carrying guns. Even though there has been a surge in gun ownership in America during the pandemic, just one in five women are gun owners.

"THE MAJORITY OF THE [MASS] KILLERS WERE DISGRUNTLED WORKERS OR JILTED LOVERS WHO WERE ACTING ON A DEEP SENSE OF INJUSTICE, AND NOT MENTALLY ILL."

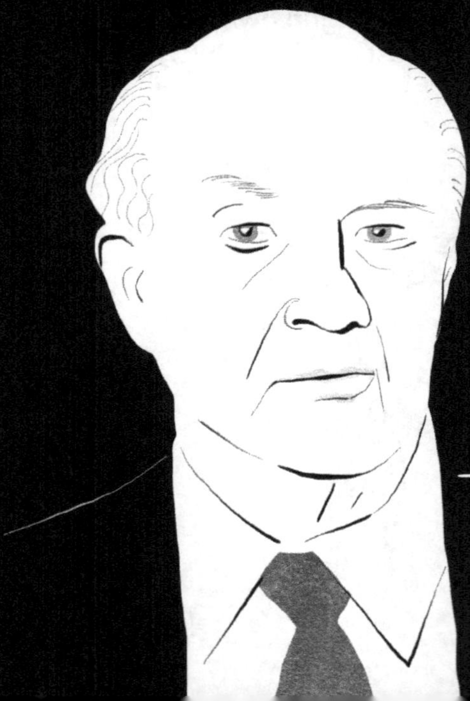

—Dr. Michael Stone,
Columbia University forensic psychiatrist

10

ROOTS OF GUN VIOLENCE

How Important Is Mental Illness?

Scholars have proposed many causes of violence, including, biological, psychological, cultural, and community factors. A great deal of evidence, including that presented in this chapter, indicates that gun ownership levels also contribute to gun violence and mortality.

SOCIAL AND ECONOMIC FACTORS

Distressed communities are those in which there is high poverty, high unemployment, many vacant housing units, many adults without a high school diploma, and few business openings.

We have found that the higher the percentage of people who live in a distressed zip code, the higher

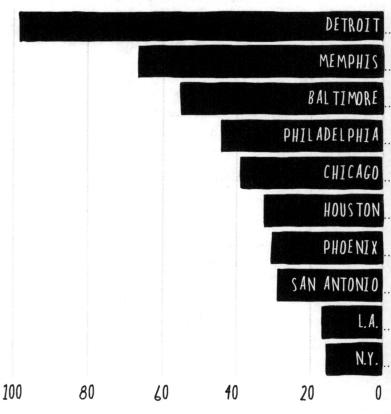

PERCENTAGE OF POPULATION IN DISTRESSED ZIP CODES

the rate of homicides and mass shootings. The table on the right shows the importance of social and economic factors in gun violence and in violence overall, as measured by the homicide rate. Cities like Detroit, Memphis, and Baltimore, in which at least half the population lives in a distressed neighborhood, have far higher homicide and mass shooting rates than cities like Los Angeles and New York, where less than a fifth of the population lives in a distressed neighborhood.

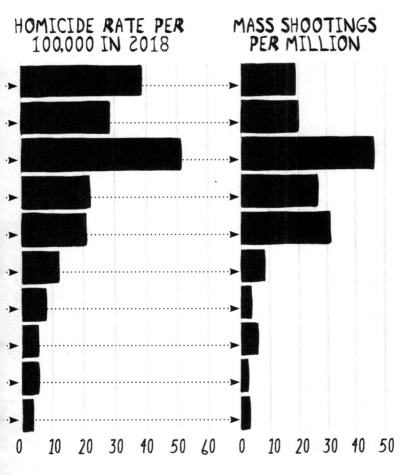

HOMICIDE RATE PER 100,000 IN 2018

MASS SHOOTINGS PER MILLION

Interviews with at-risk youth in some of New York City's toughest neighborhoods were revealing with regard to the connection between gun violence, hopelessness, and despair. Youth also mentioned the need for self-protection motivated them to carry guns.

One youth interviewed in New York noted that economic stresses led him to commit robberies and engage in drug dealing and confirmed that these activities required guns. Said one youth:

'Cause when you broke, you get angry about everything, and then you grab your gun and just do robberies and do stuff you not supposed to be doing to get your money.

A 21-year-old said gun carrying was a matter of self-preservation:

I got to keep my gun. Cops want to kill me. Dudes want to kill me. I don't know if I'll be alive tomorrow.

Another youth mentioned the code that requires an individual to retaliate if their friends are hurt:

I have to carry one [a gun]. I got beefs. They shoot at my friends. So I have to shoot back.

GUN OWNERSHIP RATES

Gun ownership rates are also important in gun violence. We have seen in Chapters 1 and 2 that the US has exceptionally high gun ownership and gun mortality rates. The odds of being murdered with a gun in a country is closely tied to levels of gun ownership.

In the same way, gun deaths in the states are closely tied to their gun ownership levels. We see that for 2014 the states with the highest gun death rates had, on average, five times the rate of gun deaths as the states with the lowest gun death rates.

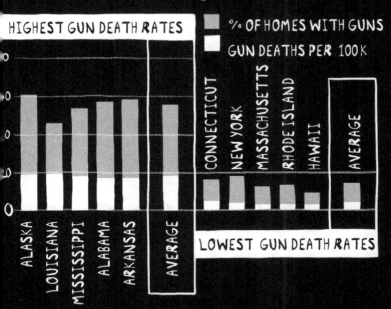

The states with the highest gun death rates on average also had four times the household gun ownership levels of the states with the fewest gun deaths.

Gun ownership is an important factor in gun deaths. States with higher gun ownership levels tend to have higher gun death rates than those with lower gun ownership levels.

STATES WITH HIGHEST AND LOWEST GUN DEATH RATES

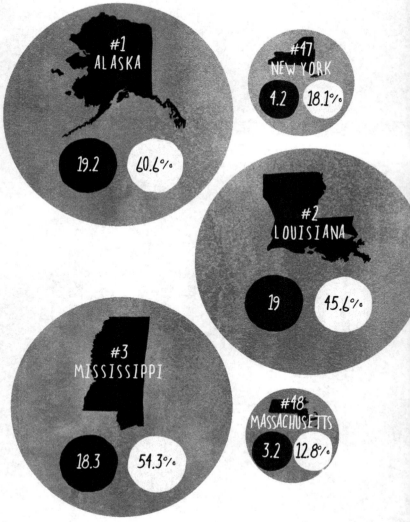

GUN DEATH RATE PER 100,000
HOUSEHOLD GUN OWNERSHIP
#4 ALABAMA
16.9
57.2%
#46 CONNECTICUT
5.0
16.2%
#5 ARKANSAS
16.6
58.3%
#50 HAWAII
2.6
9.7%
#49 RHODE ISLAND
3
13.3%
STATE AVERAGES
HIGHEST GUN DEATH RATES
18.8
55.2%
LOWEST GUN DEATH RATES
3.6
14%

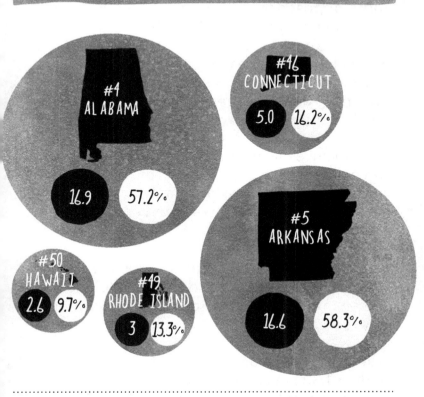

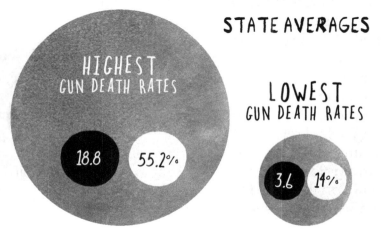

MENTAL ILLNESS AND GUN VIOLENCE

Those opposed to increasing restrictions on guns often point to mental illness as the key factor in gun violence. They claim that mass shootings and other gun violence are due to mental illness rather than a problem arising from America's high level of gun ownership and proliferation of military-grade guns. Are they right?

Gun violence can have many roots, including social and economic factors, as well as mental illness. But access to guns is also a factor as they often increase the severity of a violent attack and enable mass casualty incidents.

Serious mental illness includes conditions like schizophrenia and bipolar disorder. About four percent of violent acts are committed by a mentally ill person.

Researchers at Columbia University studied 1,800 mass murders and found that five percent are due to severe mental illness and half had no red flags that would have predicted these events. The Columbia study found that school shooters tend to be younger males who are often "nihilistic, empty, angry, feel rejected by society, blame society for their rejection, and harbor a strong desire for notoriety. They want to make their mark on the world that will elevate them to the status they believe they are entitled to and deserve."

Dr. Michael Stone, a forensic psychiatrist at Columbia University, believes that the majority of mass shooters are not mentally ill but disgruntled workers and jilted lovers with a deep sense of injustice. Most experience long-term stress due to failure at school, work, and/or relationships, blame others, and the stress builds. Then, one final life stressor can set them off.

Author Tom Gabor's study of mass shootings in 2019-2020 found that in just 1 percent of over 1,000 incidents did media reports mention that the perpetrator was mentally unstable. Most cases involved either spontaneous or ongoing disputes.

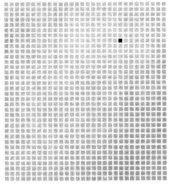

J. Reid Meloy, a forensic psychologist, states that mass shooters are not deeply ill but "injustice collectors" who are prone to perceive insults and failures as cumulative and tend to blame a person or group for their problems.

> *If you have this paranoid streak, this vigilance, this sense that others have been persecuting you for years, there's an accumulation of maltreatment and an intense urge to stop that persecution... That may never happen. The person may never act on the urge. But when they do, typically there's a triggering event. It's a loss in love or work—something that starts a clock ticking, that starts the planning.*

Severe mental illness rates do not vary much from country to country, but gun violence mortality rates do. Take schizophrenia, a serious mental illness that has not been linked to violence unless other conditions (e.g., substance abuse) are also present. While the US is in the top tier with regard to its schizophrenia prevalence rates, all countries have fewer than a half of 1 percent of their population with this diagnosis. Thus, even if there was a direct link between schizophrenia and violence, this link wouldn't explain the enormous gap in firearm homicides between the US and other high income countries.

SCHIZOPHRENIA PREVALENCE, 2019

The United States has a slightly higher schizophrenia prevalence rate than other high income countries...

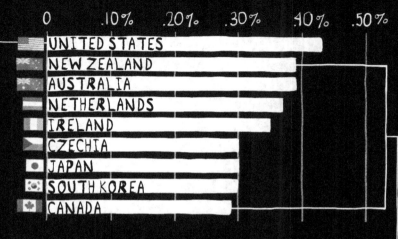

...but 25 times the gun homicide rate of these countries when they are considered together.

Psychiatrist Richard Friedman writes that psychiatry cannot protect us from mass murderers. He adds that it is difficult, if not impossible, to predict which individuals will become violent. While millions of Americans have a mental disorder or a serious anger management issue, just a minute fraction of them will commit these atrocities. Friedman argues that the focus should not be on detecting mass killers in advance, but on the availability of lethal weapons.

"THERE'S SIMPLY NO EVIDENCE OF [THE 2ND AMMENDMENT] BEING ABOUT INDIVIDUAL GUN OWNERSHIP FOR SELF-PROTECTION OR FOR HUNTING. EMPHATICALLY, THE FOCUS WAS ON THE MILITIAS."

—Michael Waldman,
constitutional scholar, author of
The Second Amendment:
a Biography

11

THE CONSTITUTION
Are Gun Rights Unlimited?

While many Americans believe that the Second Amendment to the US Constitution grants individuals the right to gun ownership, some believe that this right is unlimited. This latter segment of the population believes that the Constitution allows a person to bring any gun into any setting for any purpose and that any laws restricting the rights of gun owners violate the Constitution.

WHAT IS THE SECOND AMENDMENT?

The Second Amendment to the Constitution, part of the US Bill of Rights, was ratified in 1791. It contains the controversial reference to the right to keep and bear arms, the meaning of which is still debated vigorously today.

The Second Amendment reads:

A well regulated Militia, being necessary to the security of a free State, the right of the people to keep and bear Arms, shall not be infringed.

ARE ANY RIGHTS UNLIMITED?

No rights are without limits. Perhaps the most fundamental rights in a democracy are those relating to free speech and assembly, freedom of the press, and freedom of religion. But even these rights are not absolute. While speech is protected by the First Amendment to the US Constitution, laws that have stood for many years prohibit threats to commit physical harm, false statements that damage a person's reputation, the incitement of others to commit violence, passing on national secrets, or yelling "Fire" in a crowded theater knowing there is no fire.

Consider the following case (Schenck v. United States) in relation to speech in which the US Supreme Court clarified factors that limit people from saying anything they wish:

SCHENCK V. UNITED STATES

During World War I, activists Charles Schenck and Elizabeth Baer passed out leaflets stating that the military draft violated the Thirteenth Amendment prohibition against involuntary servitude. The leaflets urged people to disobey the draft. Schenck and Baer were charged and convicted with conspiracy to violate the Espionage Act of 1917 by encouraging insubordination in the military and obstructing recruitment. Their defense was that they were exercising their First Amendment right of free speech. In their appeal, the US Supreme Court held that the Espionage Act did not violate the First Amendment and Justice Oliver Wendell Holmes wrote that the First Amendment did not protect speech that presents a danger of a significant evil that Congress has the power to prevent.

MEANING OF THE SECOND AMENDMENT

America's first Constitution, the Articles of Confederation (1777), prohibited the formation of permanent armed forces by any state and required that each state maintain a well-regulated and disciplined militia in the event of war:

> *Every state shall always keep up a well regulated and disciplined militia, sufficiently armed and accoutred, and shall provide and constantly have ready for use, in public stores, a due number of field pieces and tents, and a proper quantity of arms, ammunition, and camp equipage.*

In the Second Amendment to America's current Constitution, a reference is made to "a well regulated Militia," a phrase used in the first Constitution to refer to militia service. Thus, it follows that the Second Amendment refers to the right to keep and bear arms for the purpose of militia service.

In his influential work on the Constitution in the 1800s, Associate Justice of the Supreme Court Joseph Story took the view that the Second Amendment's "right to keep and bear arms" referred to militias. Story wrote: "The militia is the natural defense of a free country against sudden foreign invasions, domestic insurrections, and domestic usurpations of power by rulers."

Saul Cornell, a leading historian specializing in early American and Constitutional history, has argued that the amendment was conceived to allow Americans to fulfill their civic obligation to form militias. To Cornell, the Second Amendment referred to a "civic right that guaranteed that citizens would be able to keep and bear those arms needed to meet their legal obligation to participate in a well-regulated militia."

Consistent with this interpretation, Michael Waldman, a constitutional lawyer with the Brennan Center for Justice, has argued that the Framers of the current Constitution did not consider the rights of individuals to guns outside of militia service at all when they were drafting the Second Amendment. Waldman wrote that the notes of James Madison, who drafted the Bill of Rights, including the Second Amendment, made no reference to private gun ownership, guns for self-defense, or guns for hunting at the Constitutional Convention of 1787.

In 1939 (Miller v. United States), the US Supreme Court issued its most direct ruling on the meaning of the Second Amendment to that point. Jack Miller and Frank Layton were charged in federal court with violating the National Firearms Act for transporting a sawed-off double-barrel 12-gauge shotgun across state lines. The defendants argued that the Act violated their Second Amendment right to keep and bear arms. The district court agreed and dismissed the case. In a unanimous decision, the Supreme Court reversed that decision, holding that the Second Amendment does not guarantee an individual the right to keep and bear such a weapon. Writing for the Court, Justice McReynolds reasoned:

In the absence of any evidence tending to show that possession or use of a "shotgun having a barrel of less than eighteen inches in length" at this time has some reasonable relationship to the preservation or efficiency of a well regulated militia, we cannot say that the Second Amendment guarantees the right to keep and bear such an instrument.

Former Chief Justice Warren E. Burger, a conservative, said in a 1991 interview on PBS's *MacNeil/Lehrer NewsHour* that the Second Amendment...

"...HAS BEEN THE SUBJECT OF ONE OF THE GREATEST PIECES OF FRAUD, I REPEAT THE WORD 'FRAUD,' ON THE AMERICAN PUBLIC."

He was referring to the NRA's campaign to convince Americans that the Constitution afforded every American the right to keep and bear arms. Burger quotes Elbridge Gerry, a Founding Father and eventually a vice president to James Madison, as saying that state militias served "to prevent the establishment of a standing army, the bane of liberty."

Harvard Constitutional law professor Laurence Tribe, one of America's most influential authorities on the Constitution, said popular views of law are sometimes at odds with what is on the books. Tribe says:

> *I think there are at least two constitutions of the United States. There is a kind of mythic constitution that reflects widely held beliefs, slogans. And then there is the one that starts with a piece of paper at the Archives and has an extensive history.*

Tribe notes that the Second Amendment's history and text indicate that it was intended to prevent federal interference with a state militia. He stresses the importance of the opening clause, which refers to a "well regulated Militia."

THE BREAK WITH THE PAST—2008

Dick Heller was a District of Columbia (DC) police officer who was authorized to carry a handgun while on duty. He applied for a one-year license to keep a handgun at home but his application was denied as the District had a handgun ban at the time. The District also required owners of lawfully registered firearms to keep them unloaded and disassembled or bound by a locking device unless they were located in a place of business or being used for recreational activities. Heller sued the District arguing that his Second Amendment right to keep a functional firearm in the home was violated. The district court dismissed the case but this decision was reversed by the US Court of Appeals. The US Supreme Court heard the case and, in 2008, issued its most pro-gun rights ruling to that point, establishing for the first time an individual's right to gun ownership in the home for self-defense.

THERE ARE LIMITS!

However, the conservative-majority Court made it clear that this right was not extended to everyone (felons and the mentally ill are generally prohibited from gun ownership), or to every venue (as guns can be excluded from sensitive settings like schools), or to all types of firearms ("dangerous and unusual weapons" can be prohibited). The Court asserted that limits imposed on gun ownership were in conformity with the US Constitution's Second Amendment.

Writing for the majority, Justice Antonin Scalia, a gun owner himself, stated:

> *Like most rights, the Second Amendment right is not unlimited. It is not a right to keep and carry any weapon whatsoever in any manner whatsoever and for whatever purpose: For example, concealed weapons prohibitions have been upheld under the Amendment or state analogues. The Court's opinion should not be taken to cast doubt on longstanding prohibitions on the possession of firearms by felons and the mentally ill, or laws forbidding the carrying of firearms in sensitive places such as schools and government buildings, or laws imposing conditions and qualifications on the commercial sale of arms. Miller's holding that the sorts of weapons protected are those "in common use at the time" finds support in the historical tradition of prohibiting the carrying of dangerous and unusual weapons.*

A decision of the US Supreme Court in June 2022 (Bruen ruling) further departed from 200 years of precedent by taking the view that the Second Amendment protects a right to carry guns outside the home for self-defense. The Court ruled that New York State violated the right to keep and bear arms for self-defense by requiring a person to show he had a special need for self-protection in order to obtain a permit to carry a firearm. The Court noted that the right to carry a firearm was deeply rooted in American history. However, as shown in Chapter 3, firearm regulations are also deeply rooted in US history. The Bruen decision has placed many gun laws at risk.

"THE ULTIMATE FACT IS THAT THE GUN INDUSTRY IS SIMPLY A BUSINESS, AND NOTHING MORE."

—Tom Diaz,
lawyer, former NRA member, competitive shooter, advocate for regulating the firearms industry

THE GUN INDUSTRY

The gun industry has transformed from playing a critical role in the American Revolution and other wars to a more controversial role in relation to the gun violence crisis. Together with groups like the National Rifle Association, they evolved into a powerful political lobby that has aggressively aimed to expand gun rights while blocking the most basic restrictions on guns, including those shown to prevent gun violence.

THE FIREARMS INDUSTRY IS AS OLD AS AMERICA ITSELF

The American firearms industry can be traced back to the founding in 1777 of the Springfield Armory in Springfield, Massachusetts. The armory was established as a safe place for the revolutionary forces to make and store arms. It produced military weapons used by Union soldiers during the Civil War and the M-1 Garand, the standard infantry rifle used in World War II. Other firms followed the Springfield Armory in making western Massachusetts and Connecticut hubs for gun manufacturing. Iconic companies, such as Colt, Sturm, Ruger & Co., Smith & Wesson, and the Winchester Repeating Arms Co. eventually set up in "Gun Valley." These companies developed products like the revolver, semiautomatic pistols, and various models of rifles, including the M-16 assault rifle. Following World War II, manufacturing firms were established in California and other parts of the country.

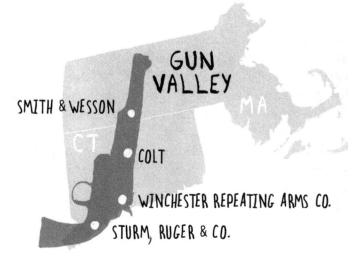

THE BUSINESS OF GUNS

The firearms industry often portrays itself as a champion of individual rights, self-reliance, and the Second Amendment. However, Tom Diaz, a lawyer, former NRA member, and competitive shooter who became an advocate for regulating the firearms industry, has made the following observation:

> *The ultimate fact is that the gun industry is simply a business, and nothing more. It is neither a national trust nor a repository of American values. Although the people who make, import, and sell guns often wrap themselves in ideological and nostalgic symbols of early America...*

...they are not latter-day founding fathers. They are businessmen. They are in the game because they want to make money, and as much of it as possible.

117

Pamela Haag, author of *The Gunning of America*, also found in her deep dive into the world of gun-makers that their priority was selling guns as a profitable item rather than one having almost a religious significance:

> *What sort of men made the guns that made the gun culture? Men who weren't inordinately or single-mindedly interested in guns… The gun-industrial elite did not aspire to invent a gun, per se. Not Eli Whitney, who moved from nails to hat pins to a government musket contract that allowed him to keep his workforce employed and machines running… Not Christopher Spencer who went from silk to guns and back to silk; who after…his failure at making guns in Paterson, New Jersey, ventured into making submarine battery prototypes before returning to the revolver. And not Oliver Winchester, who might as easily have been the men's shirt king as rifle king. They were all, in Colt's terms, principally dedicated to "making something to sell."*

Several decades ago, William Ruger Sr., chairman of Sturm, Ruger & Co., a leading manufacturer of handguns and rifles, stated:

> *We've woken up to the fact that these guns are not wearing out, and used guns are competing with our new production. People are buying guns for half the money. I think that hurt sales of a lot of companies in the 1980s.*

Ruger argued that one aspect of the solution to a saturated market was to develop innovative designs that would appeal to every gun owner. The goal was to generate a demand for products through advertising and by making guns that were more lethal, more compact, and thereby more concealable. In the 1990s and beyond, sales of semiautomatic rifles (like the AR-15) and pistols grew while the rest of the market stagnated, and these weapons encouraged "spray and pray" shooting techniques due to high-capacity magazines. These weapons were intended as a stimulus to a lethargic market rather than due to market demand.

Author Pamela Haag notes that as guns were becoming less useful tools, due to the decline of hunting and small-scale farming, companies like Winchester instructed their sales force to seduce otherwise indifferent customers who had little need for firearms as tools. She writes:

> One answer to the question: "Why do Americans love guns?" is, simply, we were invited to do so by those who made and sold them at the moment their products had shed much of their more practical, utilitarian value. What was once needed now had to be loved.

The firearms industry is very secretive and most companies are privately owned rather than publicly traded. A number of companies active in the US are subsidiaries of foreign companies. Detailed data are not available on the number of different types of firearms made and imported into the US. This said, the NSSF, the firearm industry trade association, states that the industry directly and indirectly creates about 393,000 jobs and generates $81 billion in economic activity each year.

THE GUN INDUSTRY'S LEGAL IMMUNUTY

The Protection of Lawful Commerce in Arms Act of 2005 (PLCAA) shields gun manufacturers from liability, meaning they cannot be sued when their products are used to commit acts of violence. Several cities, including New York and Chicago, had filed lawsuits against gun makers and dealers, claiming that their actions had compromised public health and created an enormous financial burden for the municipalities arising from the medical costs incurred by gun violence victims.

The PLCAA gave the gun industry unprecedented immunity from negligence-based lawsuits. Specifically, this act shields the industry from lawsuits relating to the use of firearms and ammunition, when "the product functioned as designed and intended." The act provides broad protection to companies in the gun industry that make unsafe products and engage in distribution practices that result in easy access by criminals. No other industry benefits from such protection. Removing this legal shield by repealing PLCAA would allow thousands of shooting victims and their families to sue the industry for making and marketing products that enable serious harms. Such lawsuits might lead gun-makers and dealers to conclude that it is not in their interest to sell weapons designed to produce mass casualties.

Tom Diaz, in his detailed exposé of the gun industry, noted in 1999:

> *Over the last two decades, at least, the gun industry has deliberately enhanced its profits by increasing the lethality—the killing power—of its products. Lethality is the nicotine of the gun industry. Time and time again, the gun industry has injected into the civilian market new guns that are specifically designed to be better at killing—guns with greater ammunition capacity, higher firepower in the form of bigger caliber or power, increased concealability, or all three—and created demand for these new products with the collaboration of the "gun press" and the entertainment media.*

It is ironic that, due to stricter laws in other countries, foreign manufacturers are often unable to sell to their own civilian population and export most of their products to the US. In the 1990s, for example, just over 1 percent of Japan's gun production stayed in Japan and 80 percent of the production of its three leading gun manufacturers came to the US.

GUN DEALERS AND CRIME

In 2022, there were nearly 78,000 licensed gun dealers in the US—more than all the McDonald's, Burger King, Wendy's and Subway restaurants combined. Most guns are made by licensed manufacturers and then shipped to a licensed dealer. Still, some guns make their way into the hands of individuals prohibited from gun possession and/or are used in crime.

Often, purchases are made through "straw purchasers," individuals with clean criminal records who buy guns on behalf of those who would be ineligible due to a felony conviction or some other disqualifying condition.

Some dealers are especially prolific in selling guns that are eventually used in crime. A 2000 report by the Bureau of Alcohol, Tobacco, Firearms, and Explosives (ATF) revealed that just over 1 percent of federally licensed firearm dealers sold more than half the guns later traced to crime. For example, in 2005,

447 guns used in crime were traced to a sporting goods store outside of Oakland, California. One of every eight guns sold in that store were later found to be used in a crime or were seized from an individual involved in crime.

Gun shows are another major source of crime guns.

ATF records show that **nearly a third** of guns involved in federal gun trafficking investigations have a gun show connection.

New York City investigators visited seven gun shows in three states. Their integrity tests of 47 licensed dealers and private sellers showed that **nearly two-thirds** sold to a purchaser who said he probably could not pass a background check.

More than **nine out of 10** licensed dealers sold to apparent straw purchasers.

In all, **35 out of 47** sellers approached by investigators completed sales to people who appeared to be criminals or straw purchasers.

Investigators also learned that some private sellers were in the business of selling guns without a license.

123

Major flaws or weaknesses in federal gun laws impede the ATF from preventing the illegal diversion of firearms from licensed firearm dealers. The agency is limited to one unannounced dealer inspection per year, and it faces an uphill battle in convicting dealers of wrongdoing. In criminal cases, it must show that the dealer willfully engaged in wrongdoing—a tall order—and, to revoke a license, a pattern of wrongdoing over many years must be demonstrated.

Missing records can hide illegal sales that can compromise public safety; however, serious recordkeeping violations usually go unpunished. Since 1986, recordkeeping violations are classified as misdemeanors rather than felonies and federal prosecutors do not tend to spend their limited resources prosecuting misdemeanors.

The ATF lacks the workforce to monitor the large number of gun dealers across the country. The Department of Justice's Office of the Inspector General concluded that it would take the ATF over 22 years to inspect all federally licensed dealers and, on average, dealers are inspected just once a decade. There are only about 15 license revocations in a typical year.

THE GUN LOBBY

While experiencing scandal and declining membership in the last few years, the National Rifle Association (NRA) has been one of America's most formidable political lobby groups. The NRA was formed in 1871 as Union veterans Colonel William Church and General George Wingate were troubled by the lack of marksmanship shown by their troops in the Civil War. The NRA established a rifle range in Sea Girt, New Jersey, for annual competitions and promoted the shooting sports among America's youth through the establishment of rifle clubs at major colleges, universities, and military academies. The NRA did not engage actively in lobbying until the 1960s.

In the early 1930s, following murders and crime sprees by gangsters like Al Capone and John Dillinger, sweeping bills to restrict firearms were introduced in Congress.

After the passage of the National Firearms Act of 1934, NRA President Karl Frederick stated: "I have never believed in the general practice of carrying weapons. I do not believe in the general promiscuous toting of guns. I think it should be sharply restricted and only under licenses."

Contrast this with former NRA CEO Wayne LaPierre's call in 2012 for "a cordon of security" (including armed teachers) around students following the murder of 26 elementary school children and staff at Sandy Hook Elementary School in Newtown, Connecticut:

As parents, we do everything we can to keep our children safe. It is now time for us to assume responsibility for their safety at school. The only way to stop a monster from killing our kids is to be personally involved and invested in a plan of absolute protection. The only thing that stops a bad guy with a gun is a good guy with a gun. Would you rather have your 911 call bring a good guy with a gun from a mile away...or a minute away?

In 1977, a new, radical leadership took over the NRA and the organization became one of the most effective lobby groups in America. Since then it has waged a campaign promoting the idea that the Second Amendment of the Constitution protected the right of citizens to "keep and bear arms" outside of militia service. They also waged a campaign, with the help of academic surrogates, to convince Americans that they were safer with a gun in the home and outside the home. The firearms industry is playing an increasingly influential role in shaping the activities of the organization.

David Keene, former president of the NRA, acknowledged in an interview with CNN that the organization is receiving more money from the industry than it used to and is seeking to increase these funds. The Washington-based Violence Policy Center has found that, from 2005 to 2011, corporate donations to the NRA have totaled between $20 million and $53 million. While claiming that it is independent of firearm and ammunition manufacturers and other businesses involved in the firearms industry, the reality is that a number of companies, including those making the weapons used in high-profile mass shootings have contributed million dollar gifts to the NRA. The gun industry has also sponsored NRA memberships by paying the annual dues of new members. Some NRA board members are executives of gun manufacturing firms.

For example, NRA board member Pete Brownell, owner of Brownells, which claims to be the world's largest supplier of firearms accessories and gunsmithing tools, wrote on his website:

Having [NRA] directors who intimately understand and work in leadership positions within the firearms industry ensures the NRA's focus is honed on the overall mission of the organization. These individuals bring a keen sense of the industry and of the bigger fight to the table.

The gun lobby has been highly influential in promoting or blocking a number of federal and state gun policies in the US. Policies promoted by the gun lobby include the carrying of firearms (both concealed and in the open), Stand Your Ground laws, immunizing the gun industry from lawsuits following incidents of gun violence, arming teachers, and characterizing the Second Amendment as protecting an individual right. In Florida and several other states, the lobby has even promoted a law that prevented physicians from discussing gun safety with their patients—Physician Gag Law. Such laws are enacted to ensure that doctors and other professionals do not discourage people from owning guns or emphasize the perils associated with gun possession.

"77% OF THIS FOX NEWS POLL WANT A 30-DAY WAITING PERIOD. 80% WANT RED FLAG LAWS!"

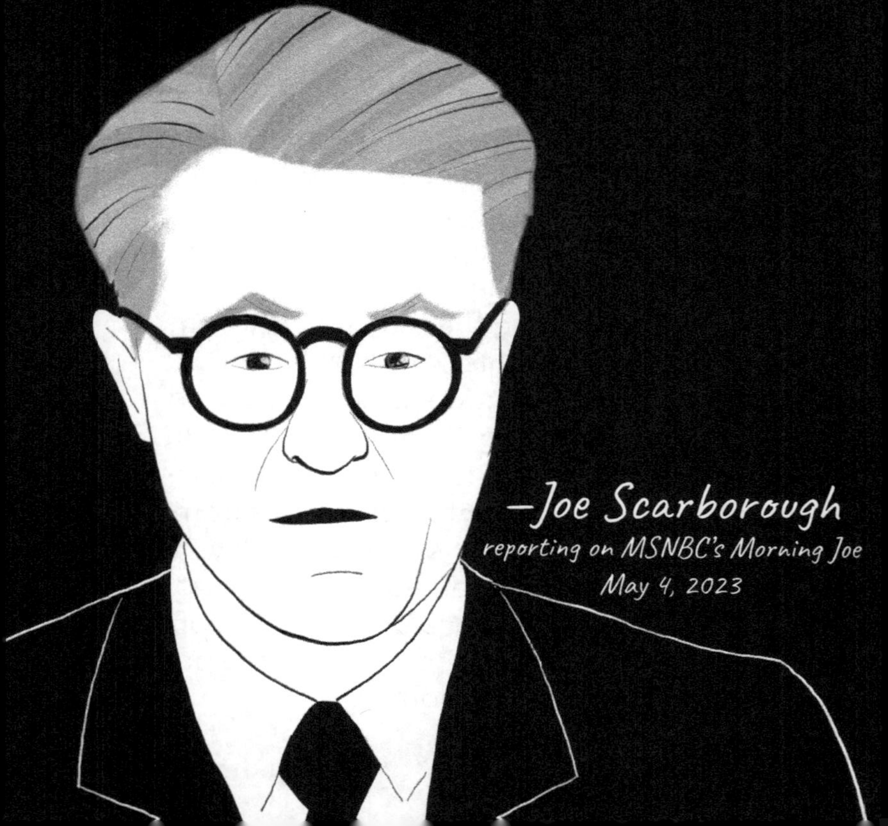

—*Joe Scarborough*
reporting on MSNBC's Morning Joe
May 4, 2023

13

PUBLIC OPINION ON GUNS AND VIOLENCE

After so many horrific mass shootings, many Americans have come to believe that significant gun law reforms will not occur in this country. Many believe that the gun lobby has too much political influence and that the public is hopelessly divided into two opposing camps: those prioritizing gun rights and those desiring stronger gun laws to reduce gun violence. However, recent polls show that many forms of regulation are supported by large majorities of Americans.

MOST AMERICANS FAVOR TOUGHER GUN LAWS

Americans are not evenly split on the issue of gun laws and gun violence. Most favor tougher laws. A recent Fox News poll found that many measures are favored by over three-quarters of Americans. Six in 10 Americans favored banning assault weapons.

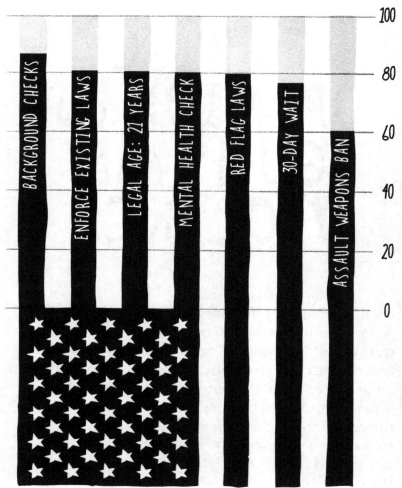

Overall, **43%** feel passing stricter gun control laws would make the country safer; a quarter feel it would make it less safe (**25%**).

A 2023 Pew Research Center poll showed that most Americans consider gun violence a serious problem, consider it too easy to get a gun, and four times as many favor stricter laws than laws that are less strict.

60% say gun violence is a major problem.

61% say it's too easy to get a gun and **9%** say it is too hard. The rest say it's about right.

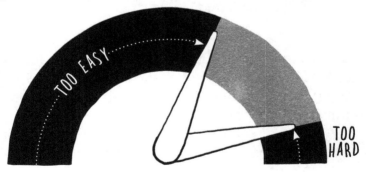

58% favor stricter gun laws and **15%** favor less strict gun laws.

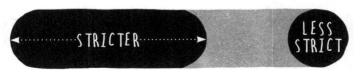

Recent Gallup polls show that close to two-thirds of Americans are not satisfied with the nation's gun laws—usually meaning they want stricter laws—and a large majority believes that easy access to guns enables mass shootings:

- **64%** are very or somewhat dissatisfied with the nation's gun laws
- **31%** are very or somewhat satisfied
- **69%** believe easy access to guns play a significant role in mass shootings

A 2018 survey conducted by researchers at Johns Hopkins University shows that gun owners and non-owners are not far apart in their support of a number of policies:

- Universal background checks were supported by **85%** of gun owners and **89%** of non-owners
- License suspension for gun dealers who cannot account for 20 or more guns in their inventory was supported by **82%** of gun owners and **86%** of non-owners
- Higher safety training standards for concealed weapon permit holders were supported by **83%** of gun owners and **85%** of non-owners

- Better reporting of mental health records for background checks was supported by *84%* of both gun owners and non-owners
- Gun prohibitions for individuals subject to temporary domestic violence restraining orders were supported by *77%* of gun owners and *82%* of non-owners
- Extreme risk protection orders for those dangerous to themselves or others (also known as red flag laws) were supported by *75%* of gun owners and *80%* of non-owners

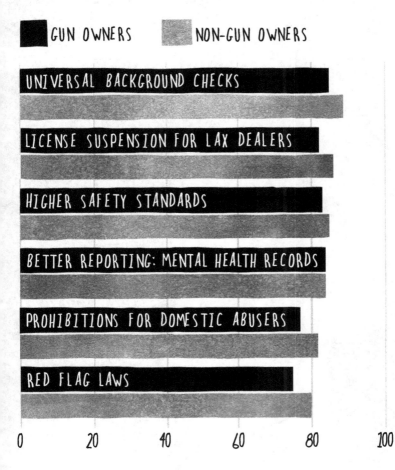

"...THE NATURE OF THE METHOD THAT IS AVAILABLE MAY HAVE A VITAL INFLUENCE ON THE OUTCOME—PARTICULARLY WHERE AN ACT IS IMPULSIVE."

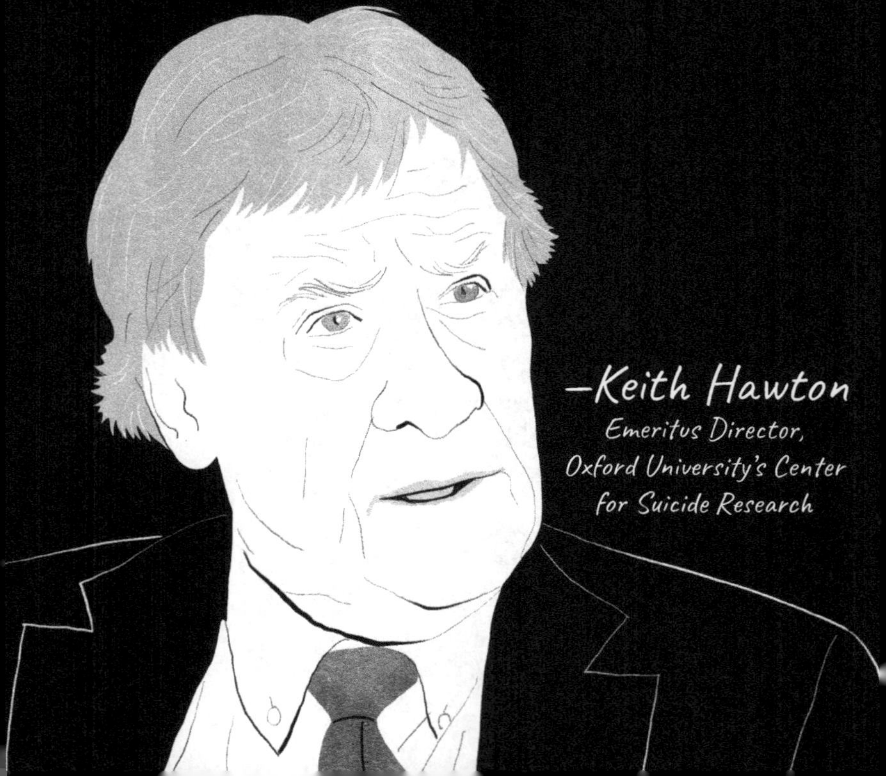

—*Keith Hawton*
Emeritus Director, Oxford University's Center for Suicide Research

SUICIDE
Do Methods Matter?

Suicides need to be considered as over half of gun deaths are intentional and self-inflicted. Suicide is considered a form of self-directed violence by the World Health Organization. As some shooters attempt or commit suicide following a homicide or mass shooting, a full discussion of gun violence cannot be undertaken without considering self-destructiveness on the part of the shooter. Interpersonal violence and suicide often go together.

LETHALITY OF SUICIDE METHODS

Research from the US, Australia, and Canada shows that the methods employed in suicide attempts vary widely in their lethality. Attempts by firearm are many times more likely to be fatal than those involving poisons, drugs, or cutting instruments. Consider a few methods examined in these studies. Firearm attempts are about 40 times as lethal as those involving cutting instruments.

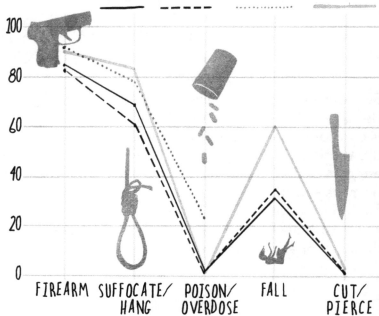

MOST ATTEMPTERS ARE NOT DETERMINED TO DIE

Kay R. Jamison, a psychologist at the Mood Disorders Center of Johns Hopkins University, estimates that just 10 to 15 percent of suicide cases involve an unwavering determination to die on the part of the victim. For the majority of suicidal people, the risk is transient. Therefore, the presence or absence of highly lethal means of ending one's life, such as firearms, at the time a person is at risk can literally make the difference between life and death. Many people do not repeat their attempts.

The following two cases illustrate the ambivalence of those who attempted suicide by jumping off the Golden Gate Bridge in San Francisco and survived:

> [Ken]Baldwin was twenty-eight and severely depressed on the August day in 1985 when he told his wife not to expect him home till late… On the [Golden Gate] bridge, Baldwin counted to ten and stayed frozen. He counted to ten again, then vaulted over. Baldwin recalls, "I instantly realized that everything in my life that I'd thought was unfixable was totally fixable–except for having just jumped."

> Kevin Hines was eighteen when he took a municipal bus to the bridge… He paced back and forth and sobbed on the bridge walkway for half an hour. No one asked him what was wrong… "So I jumped… my first thought was What the hell did I just do? I don't want to die."

METHOD AVAILABILITY AND LETHALITY ARE CRITICAL

Keith Hawton, Emeritus Director of Oxford University's Center for Suicide Research, notes that the method chosen to attempt suicide may be more important to the outcome than the individual's intent:

> *Availability of a method may be the key factor that leads to translation of suicidal thoughts into an actual suicidal act. Most importantly, the nature of the method that is available may have a vital influence on the outcome, particularly where an act is impulsive—then the person engaging in suicidal behavior is likely to use the means most easily available to them. If the method has a high risk of being fatal (e.g. firearms, dangerous chemical substances), then there is a strong possibility that the act will result in death.*

MANY SUICIDE ATTEMPTS ARE RESPONSES TO PERSONAL CRISES

In 1978, Richard Seiden, a researcher at the University of California at Berkeley published a study in which he followed up over 500 people who were prevented from attempting suicide at the Golden Gate Bridge between 1937 and 1971. An average of 26 years after the aborted attempt,

94%

94 percent of these individuals were either still alive or had died of natural causes. To Seiden, this finding supported the view that suicidal behavior is crisis-oriented and acute in nature. He concluded that if suicidal people can get through this crisis, they would be unlikely to commit suicide later.

An Alaskan study of survivors of self-inflicted gunshot wounds (mostly to the head or trunk) came to a similar conclusion. More than half of the individuals reported drinking at the time of the shooting, and many attributed the incident to the drinking. Most had no history of depression or psychiatric disorders.

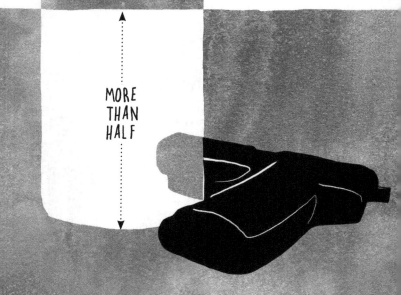

MORE THAN HALF

Many of the incidents were precipitated by a conflict with a family member or girlfriend.

"AUSTRALIA EXPERIENCED A MASSACRE AND CHANGED ITS LAWS. NEW ZEALAND HAS HAD ITS EXPERIENCE AND CHANGED ITS LAWS. I DON'T UNDERSTAND THE UNITED STATES."

—Jacinda Ardern
former Prime Minister of New Zealand

15

DO GUN LAWS WORK?

Laws do more than serve as a deterrent to those who would consider committing certain crimes. Laws codify society's values. They serve as an expression of society's revulsion toward or disapproval of certain acts and draw the line at what is unacceptable.

A FALSE AND DANGEROUS IDEA

Those objecting to gun laws often argue that gun laws don't work. They say that criminals don't follow the law and law-abiding gun owners are inconvenienced in complying with these laws. These arguments can be made in relation to any law. Many perpetrators of violent crimes against women and children go undetected, but we have never heard the proposal that we should eliminate the crime of rape or those brutalizing children. We will present evidence in this chapter that many gun laws do work, even if they do not succeed in preventing all gun violence.

Aside from preventing crime, gun laws send the message that our society treats the possession of firearms and gun violence seriously. Also, punishing those violating laws reinforces the value we place on responsible gun ownership. Having no gun laws would be an invitation for people to behave in the most reckless ways with guns as there would be no consequences.

GOOD GUYS, BAD GUYS: A FALSE DICHOTOMY

The idea that society can be neatly divided into good and bad guys is false. Many mass shooters were "good guys" without criminal records until they committed horrific crimes, including the perpetrator of the deadliest mass killing in US history in Las Vegas. We have no way of knowing who the next shooter might be without the benefit of hindsight. Many "good guys" with carry permits went on to commit violent crimes, including murder. People must be presumed innocent until they commit a crime and therefore we cannot selectively apply laws just to the "bad guys."

EVIDENCE THAT GUN LAWS CAN WORK

While laws do not deter everyone who contemplates committing a certain crime, they dissuade or thwart others. Since the introduction of the federal background check system in 1994, 4.5 million Americans were denied the ability to purchase a gun, showing that even those ineligible to buy a gun may try to do so through a licensed dealer rather than through illegal channels. Not everyone (think of teenagers committing school shootings) will have easy access to guns through such illegal networks.

Gun laws aren't just aimed at criminal behavior. They can potentially reduce suicides—over half of gun deaths—as well as deadly accidents.

Some of the strongest evidence that gun laws make an enormous difference can be found when we compare states with the strongest and weakest gun laws. The group Everytown for Gun Safety ranked how each state stacked up in relation to 50 different gun safety laws. Then they examined the firearm death rate for each state. The study found that a group of eight states with the strongest gun laws had just a third of the gun deaths per 100,000 population when compared to the 14 states with the weakest gun laws.

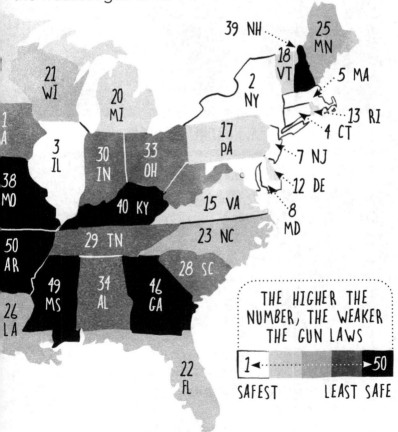

LAWS AND PROGRAMS THAT WORK

CRIMINAL BACKGROUND CHECKS

- 4.5 million people were denied a firearm transfer or permit since 1994, **a third of whom had felony records**
- States without universal background check laws export crime guns across state lines at a 30% **higher rate than states requiring background checks on all gun sales**

RATE OF EXPORTING CRIME GUNS ACROSS STATE LINES

| STATES WITH BACKGROUND CHECKS |
| STATES WITHOUT BACKGROUND CHECKS | 30% HIGHER

ASSAULT WEAPONS BAN

- Assault weapons were used in the seven deadliest mass shootings in last decade
- Assault weapons increase fatalities in mass shootings
- Mass shooting fatalities **declined by 70% during 1994-2004 federal assault weapons ban**

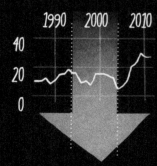

LICENSING OF GUN OWNERS

A **CONNECTICUT** licensing law was associated with major reductions in firearm homicide & suicide rates.

MISSOURI's repeal of its licensing law was followed by major increases in its firearm homicide & suicide rates.

In **80** large urban counties, licensing laws were associated with

11% a decrease in firearm homicides.

SAFE STORAGE LAWS

- 70% - 90% of guns used in youth suicides, unintentional shootings among children, and school shootings are from home of shooter, relative, or friend
- Risk of suicide & unintentional shootings among youth increases in homes where guns are kept loaded and/or unlocked

RED FLAG (EXTREME RISK) LAWS

Red flag laws allow for the temporary removal of firearms from individuals at risk of harming others or themselves.

The FBI found that the average active shooter displayed four to five concerning behaviors prior to their attack.

A study of six states with red flag laws found that 10 percent of cases involved threats of mass violence. **The laws in these states prevented more than 650 potential mass shooting incidents.**

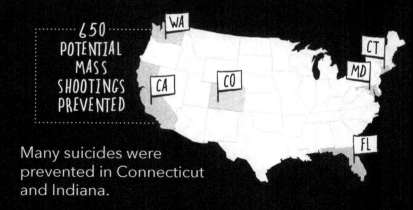

Many suicides were prevented in Connecticut and Indiana.

VIOLENCE INTERRUPTION PROGRAMS

These programs aim to prevent retaliation by victims of violence. They also provide job training, housing, and drug counseling. They have dramatically reduced arrest and reinjury in Oakland and Baltimore.

FOCUSED DETERRENCE STRATEGIES

This multiagency approach targets repeat offenders with strict enforcement and improved access to support. These programs have been associated with a moderate overall reduction in crime.

OTHER COUNTRIES DEMONSTRATE THE BENEFITS OF STRONGER GUN LAWS— JAPAN AND AUSTRALIA

There are enormous differences between the US and Japan in terms of gun-related carnage. Japan, which has almost half of the US's population, usually has fewer than 10 gun deaths per year. By contrast, the US toll in recent years has ranged between 40,000 and 50,000 annual gun deaths. While there are social and cultural differences between the two countries, the different approaches to firearm regulation are dramatic.

While current interpretations of the Second Amendment treat gun ownership as an entitlement for all Americans who are not convicted felons or deemed mentally defective, Japan embraces a policy in which the aim is to minimize the number of guns in circulation and in which numerous hurdles are created for those wishing to own guns.

To own a long gun—handguns are prohibited—in Japan, the individual must...

- Attend an all-day class
- Pass a written test
- Achieve at least 95 percent accuracy at a shooting-range test
- Pass a mental health evaluation
- Pass a background check, including a criminal record check and interviews with friends and family
- Retake the class and initial exam every three years

Gun ownership in Japan is also limited by capping the number of gun shops at three per prefecture (political district). Prefectures range from half a million to 12 million people.

In addition, new ammunition magazines can only be purchased by trading in old ones. And relatives of deceased gun owners must surrender the owner's guns.

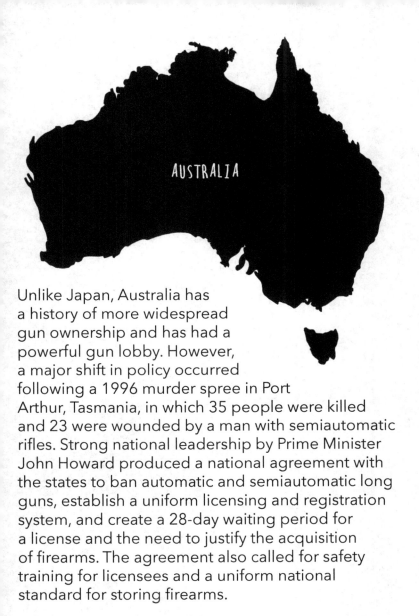

Unlike Japan, Australia has a history of more widespread gun ownership and has had a powerful gun lobby. However, a major shift in policy occurred following a 1996 murder spree in Port Arthur, Tasmania, in which 35 people were killed and 23 were wounded by a man with semiautomatic rifles. Strong national leadership by Prime Minister John Howard produced a national agreement with the states to ban automatic and semiautomatic long guns, establish a uniform licensing and registration system, and create a 28-day waiting period for a license and the need to justify the acquisition of firearms. The agreement also called for safety training for licensees and a uniform national standard for storing firearms.

Mass shootings declined following the enactment of the new policy and most observers agree that the national agreement resulted in reductions in both firearm homicides and suicides.

"THE FACT THAT WE DECIDED COLLECTIVELY THAT WE'RE OKAY WITH NOT REGULATING WEAPONS OF MASS DESTRUCTION... ASTONISHES ME EVERY SINGLE DAY."

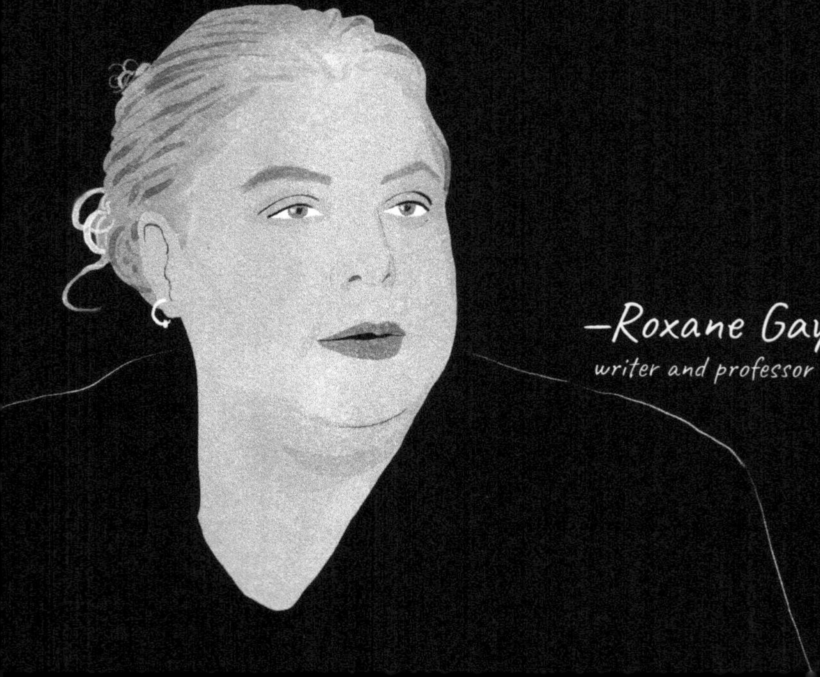

—*Roxane Gay*
writer and professor

16

A DECLARATION OF THE RIGHT OF AMERICANS TO LIVE FREE FROM GUN VIOLENCE

Drafted by Thomas Gabor

NEED FOR A CITIZEN'S BILL OF RIGHTS EMPHASIZING FREEDOM FROM GUN VIOLENCE

While much has been written and debated about the Second Amendment of the US Constitution and the extent to which it protects gun rights, little has been written about the responsibility of federal and state governments to protect their residents from unrelenting attacks on the lives and liberties of citizens by individuals wielding guns.

Legal scholars point out that protecting citizens from harm is a fundamental part of the social contract between citizens and their government. Citizens pay taxes, obey laws, and perform military service where necessary and the government provides protection from violence. Governments have failed Americans as annual gun deaths have approached 50,000 in the last few years, with many more injured.

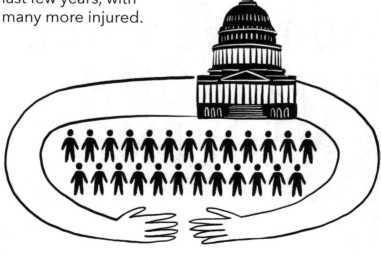

There are now nearly two mass shootings per day.

SUN	MON	TUE	WED	THU	FRI	SAT
✗ ✗	✗ ✗	✗ ✗	✗ ✗	✗ ✗	✗ ✗	✗ ✗

Currently, all Americans are vulnerable to gun violence, whether they live in large cities, small towns, or rural areas. Young people are very concerned about school shootings. There are few safe spaces in America, as so many venues have experienced mass shootings, including schools, college campuses, night clubs, theaters, libraries, airports, outdoor concerts, places of worship, shopping malls, baseball diamonds, newsrooms, and military bases. Over half of all Americans have been personally affected by gun violence and close to a third have considered avoiding certain public spaces due to their fear of gun violence.

The United States is a signatory to the Universal Declaration of Human Rights, which affirms that "Everyone has the right to life, liberty, and the security of person." The Declaration of Independence affirmed the right to life, liberty, and pursuit of happiness.

The US Supreme Court in District of Columbia v. Heller (2008) made it clear that the Second Amendment right to "keep and bear arms" was not unlimited and that laws regulating the carrying of firearms in sensitive places, denying gun ownership to "felons and the mentally ill," and "prohibiting the carrying of "dangerous and unusual weapons" did not violate the Second Amendment.

A DECLARATION OF THE RIGHT OF AMERICANS TO LIVE FREE FROM GUN VIOLENCE

This Declaration affirms that, as argued above, the federal and state governments have the duty to protect Americans from gun violence:

The People have the right to feel safe in their homes, at work, and in public spaces;

The People have the right to be in gun-free environments while in school and college;

The People have a First Amendment right to express their opinions on all subjects free of intimidation by citizens with guns, both at public gatherings and in educational environments;

The People have the right to move about, shop, work, and enjoy leisure activities in their communities without a fear of gun violence;

The People have the right to enjoy shows, sporting events, movies, and concerts without the presence of armed citizens (other than police) with guns;

The People have the right to use public transportation and to enter terminals without a fear of gun violence;

The People have the right to attend church, temples, mosques, and other places of worship without the presence of citizens with guns;

The People should be spared the harms, economic costs, and traumas associated with gun violence.

ACKNOWLEDGMENTS

This book represents a special collaboration between Tom Gabor and Violet Lemay. Their complementary skill sets have enabled them to produce this unique and original, illustrated book on gun violence that distinguishes fact from fiction.

In his 30+ years studying, teaching, and writing about gun policy, Tom has had the opportunity to meet national media figures, members of Congress, White House officials, survivors, leading activists, religious leaders, teachers, firearm dealers and trainers, and citizens with a range of views on the subject. He has learned much from these interactions and has concluded that widespread misinformation about gun violence is a major impediment to tackling this issue successfully and that books like this one must therefore counter the myths and the lies.

FROM TOM

Above all, I am very grateful for my wife Christene's love and support. She is the wind beneath my wings.

FROM VIOLET

I'd like to thank my son, Graham, who has grown up to become a solid sounding board full of good advice. I hope he can say the same about me.

Most of all, I must thank my husband, travel buddy and best friend, Fred, who celebrates my inability to let go of any creative inspiration, no matter how big or small. Fred is a brilliant designer, painter, and problem solver. He also feeds me and makes me laugh—so, yeah, he's pretty much perfect. Thanks, Babe.

NOTES

1 AMERICA'S PRIVATE ARSENAL

vii	**"Firearm violence is an urgent public health crisis":** Dr. Vivek Murthy, "U.S. Surgeon General Issues Advisory on the Public Health Crisis of Firearm Violence in the United States," US Department of Health and Human Services, bit.ly/MurthyWarning
xvi	**Photos:** Taken by Violet Lemay at a truck stop in Columbia, Missouri.
xviii	**"Few Australians would deny":** John Howard, "I Went After Guns. Obama Can, Too." *The New York Times*, January 16, 2013, www.nytimes.com/2013/01/17/opinion/australia-banned-assault-weapons-america-can too.html
1	**Americans own approximately 400 million firearms:** Aaron Karp, *Estimating Global Civilian-Held Firearms Numbers* (Geneva: Small Arms Survey, 2018), bit.ly/4fDcgl5
2	**By contrast, residents of Indonesia and Japan:** Karp, 3.
3	**Top 10 Countries:** Karp, 4.
4	**The number of assault rifles in civilian hands:** Steve Kraske and Elizabeth Ruiz, "U.S. Civilians Own an Estimated 20 million AR-15s. How the Rifle Became a Political Symbol," NPR, September 29, 2023, bit.ly/4dHePk7
5	**The National Instant Criminal Background Check System:** FBI, Firearms Checks (NICS), bit.ly/4dAfcNs
7	**Still, gun laws are far stricter:** Parliament of Australia, "Australian Gun Laws", bit.ly/AussieGunLaws
8	**All states now allow the carrying:** Giffords Law Center to Prevent Gun Violence, *Concealed Carry*, bit.ly/ConcealedCarry_Giffords
8	**Over half the states and counting:** Chip Brownlee, "Permitless Carry. These States Allow Gun Owners to Carry Without a License," *The Trace*, May 12, 2023, bit.ly/PermitlessCarry_
9	**Carrying Guns in Canada:** Dylan Matthews, "Here's How Gun Control Works in Canada," *Vox*, October 24, 2014, bit.ly/GunCarry_Canada
10	**About five million American children:** Deborah Azrael, Johanna Cohen, Carmel Sahi, Matthew Miller, "Firearm Storage in Gun-Owning Households with Children: Results of a 2015 National Survey," *Journal of Urban Health*, May 10, 2018, bit.ly/SafeStorage_Kids
10	**As Americans today are more likely:** Rajeev Ramchand, "Personal Firearm Storage in the United States," *Rand Corporation*, July 11, 2022, bit.ly/PersonalFirearmStorage
11	**Firearm storage in Germany:** Federal Ministry of Justice, *Weapons Act*, Sections 36 and 53, bit.ly/FirearmStorage_German

2 GUN DEATHS AND TRAUMA: The US vs. the World

12	**"If it's not a health problem":** Garen Wintemute, "Health Professionals, Violence, and Social Change," *Annals of Internal Medicine*, 173, no. 11 (2020): bit.ly/NoHealthProblem
14	**In 2021, 48,830 people:** National Center for Health Statistics, All Injuries, *CDC*, bit.ly/48830people
14	**There are over 100,000 nonfatal:** UCDavis Health, "What You Can Do," bit.ly/100K_nonfatal
14	**Unintentional (accidental) firearm deaths:** UCDavis Health, "What You Can Do."
14	**Firearm deaths now surpass motor vehicle deaths:** National Center for Health Statistics, All Injuries, *CDC*.
15	**The US has 25 times the gun homicide rate:** Erin Grinshteyn and David Hemenway, "Violent Death Rates in the US Compared to Those of the Other High-Income Countries, 2015," *Preventive Medicine*, 123 (2019): 20.
15	**Table comparing firearm homicides and odds of being murdered by country:** Thomas Gabor, *Confronting Gun Violence in America* (London: Palgrave MacMillan, 2016), 8.
16	**The leading cause of death for Americans under 20:** Matt McGough et al., "Child and Teen Firearm Mortality in the US and Peer Countries," *Kaiser Family Foundation*, July 18, 2023, bit.ly/LeadingCause_Under20
16	**Cause of child death rankings:** McGough et al., "Child and Teen Firearm Mortality in the US and Peer Countries," Table 1.
17	**Cause of US Child Deaths:** McGough et al., Figure 1.
19	**In the US, mass shootings about doubled:** Gun Violence Archive, "Past Summary Ledgers," bit.ly/DoubledMSs
20	**Over half of Americans are personally affected:** Shannon Schumacher et al., "Americans' Experiences with Gun-Related Violence, Injuries, and Deaths," *Kaiser Family Foundation*, April 11, 2023, bit.ly/Over_Half
20	**Close to one in three Americans say:** J. Ducharme, "A Third of Americans Avoid Certain Places Because They Fear Mass Shootings," *Time*, August 15, 2019.
20	**An American Psychological Association survey:** American Psychological Association, *Stress in America: Generation Z*, October 2018.
20	**Shooting survivors under age 20:** Liz Szabo, "Children Who Survive Shootings Endure Huge Health Obstacles and Costs," *KFF Health News*, November 7, 2023, bit.ly/SurvivorsUnder20
20	**A quote from a student survivor:** Danielle Campoamor, "Opinion: An 11-Year-Old Who Survived Uvalde Says He and his friends will Never Be the Same," CNN, November 19, 2023, www.cnn.com/2023/11/19/opinions/gun-violence-uvalde-child-survivors-campoamor/index.html
21	**Her statement illustrates the devastating:** Thomas Gabor and Fred Guttenberg, *American Carnage: Shattering the Myths That Fuel Gun Violence* (Coral Gables, FL: Mango, 2023), 49.
23	**The annual cost of gun violence:** Madison Muller, "Gun Violence Costs the US $557 Billion a Year," *Time*, September 27, 2022, bit.ly/GV_AnnualCost

3 GUN LAWS IN AMERICA: A Brief History

24	**Why must we relearn:** Robert Spitzer, "Stand Your Ground Makes No Sense," *The New York Times*, May 4, 2015, bit.ly/GV_AnnualCost
26	**As early as 1686:** Spitzer, "Stand Your Ground Makes No Sense."
26	**That era was marked by strict gun laws:** Adam Winkler, *Gunfight: The Battle Over the Right to Bear Arms in America* (New York: W.W. Norton, 2013), 113.
27	**Muster rolls like this one:** Kansas Historical Society, bit.ly/MusterRoll_Photo
28	**In notorious Dodge City:** Garry Wills, *A Necessary Evil: A History of American Distrust of Government* (New York: Simon and Schuster; 1999).
28	**Photo:** Kansas Historical Society, bit.ly/Dodge_City_Photo
29	**By the early 1900s:** Spitzer, "Stand Your Ground Makes No Sense."
30-31	**Gun laws in the early 1900s (Map of US):** Mark Frassetto, "Firearms and Weapons Legislation Up To the Early 20th Century," bit.ly/1900s_GunLaws

4 GUN CULTURE IN AMERICA

32	**"This is a gun culture":** CNN, "Maher: US Has a Bad Relationship With Guns," www.cnn.com/videos/us/2012/02/28/piers-bill-maher-guns.cnn
34	**America is awash with guns:** Aaron Karp, *Estimating Global Civilian-Held Firearms Numbers.*
34	**Just one third of adults:** Kim Parker et al., "The Demographics of Gun Ownership," *Pew Research Center*, June 22, 2017, www.pewresearch.org/social-trends/2017/06/22/the-demographics-of-gun-ownership
35	**6 percent own two-thirds:** Allison Brennan, "Analysis: Fewer US Gun Owners Own More Guns," CNN, July 31, 2012, www.cnn.com/2012/07/31/politics/gun-ownership-declining/index.html
36	**Gun ownership varies greatly:** Parker et al., "The Demographics of Gun Ownership."
37	**A study covering 2016-2020:** David Correa and Nick Wilson, "Gun Violence in Rural America," *The Center for American Progress*, September 26, 2022, www.americanprogress.org/article/gun-violence-in-rural-america
38-39	**Percentage of gun owners by state:** Rand Corporation, *Gun Ownership in America*, bit.ly/GunsByState
40	**Gender:** Parker et al., "The Demographics of Gun Ownership."
40	**Racial/Ethnic Groups:** Parker et al., "The Demographics of Gun Ownership."
41	**Rural white males:** Parker et al., "The Demographics of Gun Ownership." Photo taken by Violet Lemay.
42	**Despite spikes in gun ownership:** Tom Smith and Jaesok Son, *Trends in Gun Ownership in the United States*, (Chicago: National Opinion Research Center, 2015), bit.ly/DespiteSpikes
42	**The proportion of households involved in hunting:** Smith and Son, *Trends in Gun Ownership in the United States.*

43	**Those citing self-protection:** Sara Goo, "Why Own a Gun? Protection is Now Top Reason," *Pew Research Center,* May 9, 2013, www.pewresearch.org/fact-tank/2013/05/09/why-own-a-gunprotection-is-now-top-reason/; Katherine Schaeffer, "Key Facts About Americans and Guns," *Pew Research Center,* September 13, 2023, www.pewresearch.org/short-reads/2023/09/13/key-facts-about-americans-and-guns/
43	**While increasing noticeably, just 8 percent:** Ali Rowhani-Rahbar, "Trend in Loaded Handgun Carrying Among Adult Handgun Owners in the United States, 2015-2019," *American Journal of Public Health*, 112, no. 12 (2022): 1783.
44	**More than six times as many Americans:** Katherine Schaeffer, "Key Facts About Americans and Guns."
45	**Six in 10 Americans favor:** Schaeffer, "Key Facts About Americans and Guns."

5 GUNS DO KILL: The Weapon Matters

46	**"I keep hearing this":** "Questions for Ozzy Osbourne," *The New York Times Magazine,* June 28, 1998, www.nytimes.com/1998/06/28/magazine/sunday-june-28-1998-questions-for-ozzy-osbourne.html
49	**Dr. Arthur Kellermann, a renowned:** Arthur Kellermann et al., "The Epidemiologic Basis for the Prevention of Firearm Injuries," *Annual Review of Public Health* 12 (1991): 17.
50	**Dr. Joseph Sakran, a trauma surgeon:** N. Kirkpatrick, Atthar Mirza, Manuel Canales, "American Icon: The Blast Effect," *The Washington Post*, March 27, 2023, www.washingtonpost.com/nation/interactive/2023/ar-15-damage-to-human-body
51	**A large study of robberies:** Philip Cook, "Robbery Violence," *Journal of Criminal Law and Criminology* 78, no. 2 (1987): 357.
51	**A study using Chicago Police data:** Franklin Zimring, "Is Gun Control Likely to Reduce Violent Killings?" *University of Chicago Law Review* 35, no. 4 (1968): 721.
52	**Dayton's police chief, Richard Biehl:** Bryn Caswell, "Dayton Police Chief Richard Biehl Presents at US Secret Service Mass Attack Seminar," *Dayton Now,* August 6, 2020, bit.ly/DaytonChief
53	**All American presidential assassinations:** Oleksandra Mamchii, "US Presidents That Were Assassinated," *Best Diplomats,* May 11, 2024, bit.ly/Pres_Assassinations
53	**In 2021, of law enforcement officers:** National Law Enforcement Memorial Fund, *2021 End of Year Preliminary Law Enforcement Officers Fatalities Report,* bit.ly/PoliceFatalities

6 LETHALITY OF TODAY'S WEAPONS

54	**"Civilian sales were never the intended purpose":** TFB, "Breaking: Jim Sullivan, AR-15 Designer Makes Some Controversial Statements on HBO Tonight," *TheFirearmBlog.com,* May 24, 2016, bit.ly/JimSullivan_Quote
56	**Armalite, Inc. first developed the AR-15:** Greg Myre, "A Brief History of the AR-15," NPR, February 28, 2018, bit.ly/AR15_History
56	**"Now you can buy a hot combat rifle":** Ad appearing in Popular Science Magazine, February 1965, bit.ly/RifleAd

57	**Responding to questions about the role of these firearms:** TFB, "Breaking: Jim Sullivan, AR-15 Designer Makes Some Controversial Statements on HBO Tonight."
57	**Cameron McWhirter and Zusha Elinson, national reporters:** Cameron McWhirter and Zusha Elinson, *American Gun: The True Story of the AR-15*, (New York: Farrar, Straus and Giroux, 2023).
57	**The Sporter looks like, feels like:** Alex Horton, Monique Woo, and Tucker Harris, "American Icon," *The Washington Post,* March 27, 2023, www.washingtonpost.com/business/interactive/2023/history-of-ar-15-marketing
58	**Brown Bess Revolutionary War Musket:** Kevin Baez, "Weapons of War (1600-1800)," *Smithsonian Learning Lab,* learninglab.si.edu/collections/weapons-of-war-1600-1800/HUoHq60eaAj1UKyz
59	**AR-15:** C.A. Bridges, "Is An AR-15 an Assault Rifle? What You Need to Know About America's Most Popular Rifle," *News-Press,* June 1, 2022, www.news-press.com/story/news/local/2022/06/01/ar-15-what-it-is-what-it-can-do-and-why-so-many-mass-shooters-like-them/7467147001
60	**All of the top 10 deadliest mass shootings:** Mark Abadi et al., "The 30 Deadliest Mass Shootings in Modern US History Include Monterey Park and Uvalde," *Business Insider,* January 23, 2023, bit.ly/Worst_MSs
62	**Weisser adds:** Michael Weisser, *Gun Myths* (Ware, MA: Tee Tee Press, 2021), 35-36.
63	**A Boston study demonstrates the greater lethality:** Anthony Braga and Philip Cook, "The Association of Firearm Caliber with Likelihood of Death From Gunshot Injury in Criminal Assaults," *JAMA Network Open,* July 7, 2018.

7 SELF-DEFENSE : Reality or Illusion?

64	**"The only thing that stops…":** Peter Overby, NRA: "The Only Thing That Stops a Bad Guy With a Gun is a Good Guy With a Gun," NPR, December 21, 2012, www.npr.org/2012/12/21/167824766/nra-only-thing-that-stops-a-bad-guy-with-a-gun-is-a-good-guy-with-a-gun
66	**Armed self-defense advocates often refer:** Gary Kleck and Mark Gertz, "Armed Resistance to Crime: The Prevalence and Nature of Self-Defense with a Gun," *Journal of Criminal Law and Criminology* 86 (1995): 150, bit.ly/ArmedSelfDefense
66	**A number of researchers nominate the Kleck and Gertz findings:** Philip Cook et al., "The Gun Debate's New Mythical Number: How Many Defensive Uses Per Year," *Journal of Policy Analysis and Management* 16 (1997): 463.
67	**Criminal court judges evaluated reported self-defense uses:** David Hemenway, Deborah Azrael, and Matthew Miller, "Gun Use in the United States: Results From Two National Surveys," *Injury Prevention* 6, no. 4 (2000): 263.
67	**A study of 14,000 personal contact crimes:** David Hemenway and Sara Solnick, "The Epidemiology of Self-Defense Gun Use: Evidence from the National Crime Victimization Surveys, 2007-2011," *Preventive Medicine* 79 (2015): 22. bit.ly/ContactCrimes
67	**Overall, for the years 2007-2011:** Jennifer Mascia, "How often are guns used for self-defense?" *The Trace,* June 3, 2022, bit.ly/SelfDefenseUse

68	**In 2019, FBI data showed:** FBI, *2019 Crime in the US*, Tables 14 and 20 under homicide, bit.ly/FBI_Table14; bit.ly/FBI_Table20
69	**They found that when homes were matched:** Arthur Kellermann et al., "Gun Ownership as a Risk Factor for Homicide in the Home," *New England Journal of Medicine* 329 (1993): 1084, bit.ly/HomeHomicide
69	**In another study led by Dr. Kellermann:** Arthur Kellermann et al., "Injuries and Deaths Due to Firearms in the Home," *Journal of Trauma* 45 (1998): 263, bit.ly/HomeAccidents
70	**An FBI study of 333 of these incidents:** Federal Bureau of Investigation, "Active Shooter Incidents: 20-Year Review 2000-2019," *Department of Justice*, bit.ly/ActiveShooter_Incidents
70	**Dallas' Chief Brown stated:** Molly Hennessey-Fiske, "Dallas Police Chief: Open Carry Makes Things Confusing During Mass Shootings," *Los Angeles Times*, July 11, 2016, www.latimes.com/nation/la-na-dallas-chief-20160711-snap-story.html
71	**Professor John Donohue and his colleagues:** John J. Donohue, Abhay Aneja and Kyle D. Weber, "Right-to-Carry Laws and Violent Crime: A Comprehensive Assessment Using Penal Data and a State-Level Synthetic Control Analysis," *Journal of Empirical Legal Studies* 16 (2019): 198.
71	**A Harvard University survey found:** David Hemenway, Deborah Azrael, and Matthew Miller, "US National Attitudes Concerning Gun Carrying," *Injury Prevention*, 7, no. 4 (2001): 282.
72	**With surging gun carrying in recent years:** Jennifer Mascia and Chip Brownlee, "Road Rage Shootings Have surged Over the Past Decade," *The Trace*, April 25, 2024, bit.ly/RoadRage_Guns
74	**Florida's SYG law was associated:** David Humphreys, Antonio Gasparrini, Douglas Wiebe, "Evaluating the Impact of Florida's 'Stand Your Ground' Self-Defense Law on Homicide and Suicide by Firearm: An Interrupted Time Series Study," *JAMA Internal Medicine* 177 (2017): 44, bit.ly/SYG_Fla
74	**Homicide rates in 21 states:** Cheng Cheng, Mark Hoekstra, "Does strengthening self-defense law deter crime or escalate violence?" *The Journal of Human Resources* 48 (2013): 821, http://business.baylor.edu/Scott_Cunningham/teaching/cheng-and-hoekstra-2013.pdf
74	**In these states, a white shooter:** American Bar Association, "National Task Force on Stand Your Ground Laws. Preliminary Report and Recommendations," *American Bar Association*, 21-22.
75	**Permitless carry laws have been found:** Nick Wilson, "Fact Sheet: Weakening Requirements to Carry a Concealed Firearm Increases Violent Crime," *Center for American Progress,* October 24, 2022, www.americanprogress.org/article/fact-sheet-weakening-requirements-to-carry-a-concealed-firearm-increases-violent-crime
75	**Joseph Vince, a former agent with:** Joseph Vince, Timothy Wolfe, and Layton Field. *Firearms Training and Self-Defense* (Chicago: National Gun Victims Action Council, 2015), 4.
76	**"The average violent attack is over":** Vince et al., *Firearms Training and Self-Defense*, 19.
77	**Several studies show that, in combat situations:** Gregory Morrison, "Police Firearms Training Survey. Preliminary Findings," Paper presented at the Annual Meeting of the Academy of Criminal Justice Sciences. Anaheim, CA: March 2002.

| 77 | **Mike Weisser, a former gun dealer and trainer:** Personal communication with Mike Weisser, December 14, 2021. |

8 MASS SHOOTINGS: Random, Targeted, or Reckless?

78	**"Most mass shootings arise from arguments":** Thomas Gabor, *Carnage: Preventing Mass Shootings in America* (St. Petersburg, Florida: Booklocker, 2021).
80	**Trends in recent years show:** *Gun Violence Archive*, www.gunviolencearchive.org
80	**There is a wide variety of mass shootings:** Gabor, *Carnage: Preventing Mass Shootings in America*, 6.
81	**The New York Times reports:** Traci Angel et al., "The Kansas City Super Bowl Parade Shooting: What We Know," *The New York Times*, March 21, 2024, www.nytimes.com/article/kansas-city-parade-shooting.html
82	**In his book *Rampage Nation*:** Louis Klarevas, *Rampage Nation: Securing America from Mass Shootings* (New York: Prometheus, 2016), 161.
82	**In his book *CARNAGE*:** Gabor, *Carnage*, 87.
83	**Contagion has been observed in the case of suicides:** James Meindl and J. Ivy, "Mass Shootings: The Role of the Media in Promoting Generalized Imitation," *American Journal of Public Health*, 107, no. 3 (2017), 368.
84	**While not all studies have found evidence:** Sherry Towers et al., "Contagion in Mass Killings and School Shootings," *PLOS One*, 10, no. 7 (2015), bit.ly/MSs_Contagious
85	**Within two weeks of the Parkland (Florida):** Dixizi Liu, Zhijie Sasha Dong, and Guo Qiu, "Exploring the Contagion Effect of Social Media on Mass Shootings," *Computers and Industrial Engineering*, 172 (2022), bit.ly/MSs_SocialMedia
85	**Two of the incidents targeted:** Bill Hutchinson, "California Massacres Suggest Phenomenon of 'Mass Shooting Contagion': Experts," January 26, 2023, bit.ly/CA_MSs
85	**17 mass shootings occurred:** Liu et al., "Exploring the Contagion Effect of Social Media on Mass Shootings."

9 DO GUNS MAKE WOMEN SAFER?

86	**"A gun is not":** Caitlin Kelly, *Blown Away: American Women and Guns* (New York: Gallery Books, 2004), 92.
87	**Over nine in 10 women:** Erica L. Smith, "Female Murder Victims and Victim-Offender Relationship, 2021," *Bureau of Justice Statistics*, December 2022, bit.ly/Fem_Victims
88	**One study found that women:** Douglas Wiebe, "Homicide and Suicide Risks Associated with Firearms in the Home: A National Case-Control Study," *Annals of Emergency Medicine* 41, no. 6 (2003): 775.

88	**A homicide is eight times more likely:** Jacquelyn Campbell et al., "Risk Factors for Femicide in Abusive Relationships: Results from a Multisite Case Control Study," *American Journal of Public Health* 93, no. 7 (2003): 1089, bit.ly/AbusivePartners
88	**The trauma experienced by women who have been abused:** Susan Sorenson and Rebecca Schut, "Nonfatal Gun Use in Intimate Partner Violence: A Systematic Review of the Literature," *Trauma, Violence and Abuse* 19, no. 4 (2016), bit.ly/Abuse_Trauma
89	**Just a dozen or so women use a gun:** Violence Policy Center, *Firearm Justifiable Homicides and Non-Fatal Self-Defense Gun Use*. Washington, DC: 2019, bit.ly/Fem_GunUse
90	**She now cautions other women:** Evan Defilippis, "Having a Gun in the House Doesn't Make a Woman Safer," *The Atlantic,* February 23, 2014, bit.ly/Gun_in_House
91	**Caitlyn Kelly, an award-winning freelance writer:** Kelly, *Blown Away*, 92.
91	**Even though there has been a surge:** Parker et al., "The Demographics of Gun Ownership."

10 ROOTS OF GUN VIOLENCE : How Important Is Mental Illness?

92	**The majority of the [mass] killers:** Benedict Carey, "Are Mass Murderers Insane? Usually Not, Researchers Say," *The New York Times*, November 8, 2017, www.nytimes.com/2017/11/08/health/mass-murderers-mental-illness.html
95	**Cities like Detroit, Memphis, and Baltimore:** Gabor, *Carnage*, 53.
96	**Interviews with at-risk youth:** Rachel Swaner et al., "'Gotta Make Your Own Heaven': Guns, Safety, and the Edge of Adulthood in New York City," *Center for Court Innovation*, 2020.
97	**In the same way, gun deaths in the states:** Gabor, *Confronting Gun Violence in America*, 120.
100	**About four percent of violent acts are committed:** Kate Masters, "Media Coverage of the Mentally Ill Exaggerates Their Role in Gun Violence," *The Trace*, June 6, 2016, bit.ly/GV_MI
100	**Researchers at Columbia University studied:** Ragy Girgis, "Is There a Link Between Mental Health and Mass Shootings?" *Columbia University Department of Psychiatry,* July 6, 2022, bit.ly/MSs_MentalHealth
101	**Dr. Michael Stone, a forensic psychiatrist:** Carey, "Are Mass Murderers Insane? Usually Not, Researchers Say."
101	**Author Tom Gabor's study of mass shootings:** Gabor, *Carnage*, 91.
101	**J. Reid Maloy, a forensic psychologist:** Carey, "Are Mass Murderers Insane? Usually Not, Researchers Say."
102	**While the US is in the top tier:** Our World in Data, "Schizophrenia Prevalence," 2019, bit.ly/Schiz_TopTier
103	**Psychiatrist Richard Friedman writes that psychiatry:** Richard Friedman, "Psychiatrists Can't Stop Mass Killers," *The New York Times*, October 11, 2017, www.nytimes.com/2017/10/11/opinion/psychiatristsmass-killers.html

11 THE CONSTITUTION: Are Gun Rights Unlimited?

104	**"There's simply no evidence of [the Second Amendment]":** Hannah Levintova, "The Second Amendment Doesn't Say What You Think it Does," *Mother Jones,* June 19, 2014, bit.ly/A2_NWYT
107	**Schenck v. United States:** *Schenck v. United States,* bit.ly/Schenck_US
108	**America's First Constitution, the Articles of Confederation (1777):** The Articles of Confederation, bit.ly/1stConst
108	**Story wrote: "The militia is the natural defense":** Joseph Story, *Commentaries on the Constitution of the United States, 1833,* http://resources. utulsa.edu/law/classes/rice/Constitutional/Storey/00_story_vol1_intro.html
109	**To Cornell, the Second Amendment referred to:** Saul Cornell, *A Well Regulated Militia: The Founding Fathers and the Origins of Gun Control in America* (New York: Oxford University Press, 2006).
109	**Consistent with this interpretation, Michael Waldman:** Michael Waldman, *The Second Amendment: A Biography* (New York: Simon & Schuster, 2014), 27.
109	**Writing for the Court, Justice McReynolds reasoned:** *United States v. Miller,* 307 US 174 (1939), supreme.justia.com/cases/federal/us/307/174/
111	**Former Chief Justice Warren E. Burger, a conservative:** Interviews with Justice Warren Burger on the *MacNeil/Lehrer NewsHour,* bit.ly/WarrenBurger_ Interview
111	**Burger quotes Elbridge Gerry, a Founding Father:** "Amendments to the Constitution," *Debates Over the Bill of Rights in the First Congress,* August 17, 1789, bit.ly/Burger_Gerry
111	**Tribe says: "I think there are at least two constitutions":** Joan Biskupic, "Guns: A Second (Amendment) Look," *The Washington Post,* May 10, 1995, www.washingtonpost.com/wp-srv/national/longterm/supcourt/stories/ courtguns051095.htm
112	**The US Supreme Court heard the case:** *District of Columbia v. Heller,* 554 US 570 (2008).
113	**A decision of the US Supreme Court:** *New York State Pistol Association, Inc. et al. v. Bruen.*

12 THE GUN INDUSTRY

114	**"The ultimate fact is that":** Tom Diaz, *Making a Killing: The Business of Guns in America* (New York: The Free Press, 1999), 3.
116	**The American firearms industry can be traced:** Diaz, *Making a Killing: The Business of Guns in America,* 19.
117	**However, Tom Diaz, a lawyer:** Diaz, 3.
118	**Pamela Haag, author of *The Gunning of America*:** Pamela Haag, *The Gunning of America* (New York: Basic Books, 2016), 2.
118	**"We've woken up to the fact that these guns":** E. Eckholm, "Ailing Gun Industry Confronts Outrage Over Glut of Violence," *The New York Times,* March 8, 1992.

119	**"One answer to the question: Why do Americans love guns?":** Haag, *The Gunning of America,* xviii.
119	**This said, the NSSF, the firearm industry trade association:** NSSF, "Industry Economic Impact Up 371% Since 2008," www.nssf.org
120	**The Protection of Lawful Commerce in Arms Act:** GovInfo, *Public Law 109-92 – Protection of Lawful Commerce in Arms Act,* bit.ly/ArmsCommerce
121	**Tom Diaz, in his detailed exposé of the gun industry:** Diaz, 15.
121	**In the 1990s, for example:** Diaz, 31.
122	**In 2022, there were nearly 78,000:** Everytown for Gun Safety, *Inside the Gun Shop,* bit.ly/78Kguns
122	**A 2000 report by the Bureau of Alcohol:** Bureau of Alcohol, Firearms, Tobacco, and Explosives, *Commerce in Firearms in the United States* (Washington, DC: Department of Treasury, 2000).
122	**For example, in 2005, 447 guns:** Denis Henigan, *Lethal Logic: Exploding the Myths That Paralyze American Gun Policy* (Washington, DC: Potomac Books, 2009), 174-175.
123	**ATF records show that nearly a third:** Bureau of Alcohol, Tobacco, Firearms, and Explosives, *Following the Gun: Enforcing Federal Law Against Firearms Traffickers* (Washington, DC: US Department of the Treasury, 2000).
123	**New York City investigators visited seven gun shows:** The City of New York, "Gun Show Undercover: Report on Illegal Sales at Gun Shows," *The City of New York,* 2009.
124	**The Department of Justice's Office of the Inspector General:** Office of the Inspector General, *Inspections of Firearms Dealers by the Bureau of Alcohol, Tobacco, Firearms, and explosives.* Washington, DC: US Department of Justice, 2004, iii.
125	**After the passage of the National Firearms Act:** Michael S. Rosenwald, "The NRA Once believed in Gun Control and Had a Leader Who Pushed For It," *The Washington Post,* February 22, 2018, www.washingtonpost.com/news/retropolis/wp/2017/10/05/the-forgotten-nra-leader-who-despised-the-promiscuous-toting-of-guns
125	**Contrast this with former NRA CEO Wayne LaPierre's:** NRA, "Full Statement by Wayne LaPierre in Response to Newtown Shootings," *The Guardian,* December 21, 2012, bit.ly/LaPierre_Newton
126	**The Washington-based Violence Policy Center:** Violence Policy Center, *Blood Money: How the Gun Industry Bankrolls the NRA,* (Washington, DC: Violence Policy Center, 2011), 1.
127	**For example, NRA Board member Pete Brownell:** Violence Policy Center, *Blood Money,* 4.

13 PUBLIC OPINION ON GUNS AND VIOLENCE

| 128 | **77 percent of this Fox News poll:** Victoria Balara, "Fox News Poll: Voters favor Gun Limits Over Arming Citizens to Reduce gun Violence," *foxnews.com,* April 27, 2023, www.foxnews.com/official-polls/fox-news-poll-voters-favor-gun-limits-arming-citizens-reduce-gun-violence |

131	**A 2023 Pew Research Center poll:** Katherine Schaeffer, "Key Facts About Americans and Guns," www.pewresearch.org/short-reads/2023/09/13/key-facts-about-americans-and-guns
132	**Recent Gallup polls show that close:** Gallup, "Guns," bit.ly/Gallup_Guns
133	**A 2018 survey conducted by researchers:** Alicia Samuels, "Gun Owners and Non-Gun Owners Agree on Many Gun Safety Proposals," *Johns Hopkins University Hub*, May 17, 2018, bit.ly/SafetyProtocols_Agree

14 SUICIDE: Do Methods Matter?

134	**"The nature of the method that is available":** Keith Hawton, "Restriction of Access to Methods of Suicide as a Means of Suicide Prevention," *Prevention and Treatment of Suicidal Behavior: From Science to Practice* (Oxford: Oxford University Press, 2005), 279.
136	**Firearm attempts are about 40 times:** Gabor, *Confronting Gun Violence in America*, 94.
137	**Kay R. Jamison, a psychologist:** Kay Jamison, *Night Falls Fast: Understanding Suicide* (New York: Knopf, 1999), 47.
138	**The following two cases illustrate:** Tad Friend, "Jumpers: The Fatal Grandeur of the Golden Gate Bridge," *The New Yorker,* October 5, 2003, bit.ly/jumpers_NewYorker
139	**Keith Hawton, Emeritus Director of Oxford University's:** Hawton, "Restriction of Access to Methods of Suicide as a Means of Suicide Prevention," 279.
139	**An average of 26 years after:** Richard Seiden, "Where Are They Now: A Follow Up Study of Suicide Attempters from the Golden Gate Bridge," *Suicide and Life-Threatening Behavior*, 8, no. 4 (1978), 203.
140	**An Alaskan study of survivors:** B. Kost-Grant, "Self-inflicted Gunshot Wounds Among Alaska Natives," *Public Health Reports,* 98, no. 1 (1983), 72.

15 DO GUN LAWS WORK?

142	**"Australia experienced a massacre":** Eleanor Ainge Roy, "'I Don't Understand': Jacinda Ardern Mystified by Lack of US Gun Control," *The Guardian,* May 14, 2019, bit.ly/Ardern_Guns
145	**Many "good guys" with carry permits:** Susan Glick and Marty Langley, *License to Kill and Kidnap and Rape and Drive Drunk: An Update on Arrests of Texas Concealed Handgun License Holders* (Washington, DC: Violence Policy Center; 1999).
145	**Since the introduction of the federal:** Brady, "How Brady Background Checks Became Law," bit.ly/Brady_BGchecks
147	**The group Everytown for Gun Safety:** Everytown Research and Policy, "Gun Safety Policies Save Lives," bit.ly/safePolicies
148	**States without universal background check laws:** Daniel W. Webster, Jon S. Vernick, and Maria T. Bulzacchelli, "Effects of State-level Firearm Seller Accountability Policies on Firearm Trafficking," *Journal of Urban Health* 86, no. 4 (2009): 525.

148	**Mass shooting fatalities declined by 70 percent:** Charles DiMaggio et al., "Changes in US Mass Shooting Deaths Associated with the 1994-2004 Federal Assault Weapons Ban: Analysis of Open-source Data," *Journal of Trauma and Acute Care Surgery* 86, no. 1 (2019): 11.
149	**Licensing of gun owners:** Giffords Law Center to Prevent Gun Violence, "Licensing," bit.ly/Giffords_Licensing
149	**70 to 90 percent of guns used in youth suicides:** Renee M. Johnson, et al., "Who Are the Owners of Firearms Used in Adolescent Suicides?," *Suicide and Life-threatening Behavior* 40, no. 6 (2010): 609.
149	**Risk of suicide and unintentional shootings:** David C. Grossman, et al., "Gun Storage Practices and Risk of Youth Suicide and Unintentional Firearm Injuries," *JAMA* 293, no. 6 (2005): 707.
150	**The FBI found that the average active shooter:** James Silver, Andre Simons, and Sarah Craun, "A Study of the Pre-Attack Behaviors of Active Shooters in the United States," Federal Bureau of Investigation, June 2018, bit.ly/preAttack
150	**A study of six states with red flag laws:** April M. Zeoli, et al., "Extreme risk protection orders in response to threats of multiple victim/mass shooting in six U.S. states: A descriptive study," *Preventive Medicine* 165, part A (2022): 107304.
150	**Many suicides were prevented:** Aaron J. Kivisto and Peter Lee Phalen, "Effects of Risk-based Firearm Seizure Laws in Connecticut and Indiana on Suicide Rates, 1981-2015," *Psychiatric Services* 69, no. 8 (2018): 855.
150	**They have dramatically reduced arrest and reinjury:** Gabor, *Carnage*, 108-109.
150	**These programs have been associated:** Anthony A. Braga and David L. Weisburd, "The Effects of Focused Deterrence Strategies on Crime: A Systematic Review and Meta-Analysis of the Empirical Evidence," *Journal of Research in Crime and Delinquency*, 49, no. 3, bit.ly/DeterrenceStrategies
151	**Japan, which has almost half of the US' population:** Chris Weller et al., "Japan Has Almost Completely Eliminated Gun Deaths—Here's How," *Business Insider*, April 20, 2023, bit.ly/JapansGuns
152	**To own a long gun—handguns are prohibited:** Weller et al., "Japan Has Almost Completely Eliminated Gun Deaths—Here's How."
153	**Strong national leadership by Prime Minister John Howard:** Gabor, *Confronting Gun Violence in America*, 316-317.

16 A DECLARATION OF THE RIGHT OF AMERICANS TO LIVE FREE FROM GUN VIOLENCE

154	**"The fact that we decided":** Roxane Gay, "Considering Black Women & Gun Ownership with 'Stand Your Ground,'" *The Daily Show*, August 6, 2024, bit.ly/RoxaneGay_Guns

ABOUT THE AUTHOR

TOM GABOR earned his PhD at Ohio State University and has been a professor, researcher, and consultant in the area of gun violence for 35+ years. A criminologist and sociologist, Tom conducted the first comprehensive review of research on gun violence for the Canadian government in the early 1990s. He was an adviser to the United Nations in its study of international firearms regulation in 1998. He was retained as an expert by the families of the young victims of a mass shooting at Dunblane Primary School in Scotland in 1996. Tom submitted expert testimony to Lord Cullen's Public Inquiry into the massacre, an Inquiry that led to major changes in the United Kingdom's firearms laws. He has also advised numerous government agencies, such as Canada's Department of Justice, Public Safety Canada, Canada's Border Services Agency, and Canada's National Crime Prevention Council.

Tom's recent books include *Confronting Gun Violence in America* (2016), *ENOUGH: Solving America's Gun Violence Crisis* (2019), *CARNAGE: Preventing Mass Shootings in America* (2020), and *American Carnage* (2023), co-authored with Fred Guttenberg. He has been a contributing writer to *Fortune* magazine and is a regular opinion writer for a number of newspapers. Tom has drafted a *Declaration of the Right to Live Free from Gun Violence*, which appears in this book and affirms the right of Americans to be protected from gun violence by their government, based on America's founding documents and on international agreements signed or ratified by the US.

Tom has appeared on a variety of media programs and on numerous podcasts. He has spoken in front of numerous groups concerned about gun violence, including the League of Women Voters, Moms Demand Action for Gun Sense in America, Concert Across America, Indivisibles, March for Our Lives, Brady United Against Gun Violence, and the National Council of Jewish Women, as well as numerous faith groups, political clubs, and community organizations. For more information on his professional activities, please visit: thomasgaborbooks.com.

ABOUT THE ILLUSTRATOR

VIOLET LEMAY left her life as a theater designer in NYC to earn her master's in illustration from the Savannah College of Art and Design. She spent the first 10 years of her illustration career in the editorial market, contributing regularly to newspapers and magazines including the *Washington Post*, *The New York Times*, *Texas Monthly*, and *Psychology Today*.

When motherhood sparked Violet's interest in children's books, she shifted the focus of her career. Since then, she has illustrated nearly 50 books for kids of all ages, eight of which she also wrote.

Horrified by the Uvalde mass shooting, Violet made a social media campaign as a tribute. She created and posted portraits of each of the victims, which put her in touch with the family of student victim

Alithia Ramirez. After learning more about Alithia, Violet was inspired to write and illustrate the picture book biography *Alithia Ramirez Was an Artist*, which won many awards including Reading the West's Best Picture Book and the Hoffer Grand Prize. All author proceeds from the book fund a scholarship in Alithia's name. (For more information, please visit alithiasartangels.com.)

Subsequent anti-gun-violence social media campaigns put Violet in touch with Fred Guttenberg and Tom Gabor, authors of *American Carnage*, which led to her collaboration with Tom Gabor for this book.

Violet's books have been translated into many languages. Her illustrations have won many awards and are featured as part of the permanent collection of the Hyundai Museum of Kids' Books and Art in Seoul, Korea.

Violet is on social media @violetlemay. Please visit her website, violetlemay.com, to see what she's working on next.

Mango Publishing, established in 2014, publishes an eclectic list of books by diverse authors—both new and established voices—on topics ranging from business, personal growth, women's empowerment, LGBTQ studies, health, and spirituality to history, popular culture, time management, decluttering, lifestyle, mental wellness, aging, and sustainable living. We were recently named 2019 *and* 2020's #1 fastest growing independent publisher by *Publishers Weekly*. Our success is driven by our main goal, which is to publish high quality books that will entertain readers as well as make a positive difference in their lives.

Our readers are our most important resource; we value your input, suggestions, and ideas. We'd love to hear from you—after all, we are publishing books for you!

Please stay in touch with us and follow us at:

Facebook: Mango Publishing
Twitter: @MangoPublishing
Instagram: @MangoPublishing
LinkedIn: Mango Publishing
Pinterest: Mango Publishing
Newsletter: mangopublishinggroup.com/newsletter

Join us on Mango's journey to reinvent publishing, one book at a time.

www.ingramcontent.com/pod-product-compliance
Lightning Source LLC
Jackson TN
JSHW012326080325
80341JS00003B/3